BEYOND THE COUCH

BEYOND THE COUCH

Turning Your Behavioral Health Degree
Into Cash Without Losing Your Soul

BRYAN G. MILLER PhD

MILFORD, NEBRASKA

ISBN: 978-0-9837101-1-0
Library of Congress Control Number: 2011931888

Council Tree Press
P.O. Box 376
Milford, NE 68405
www.CouncilTreePress.com

Editor: Matthew J. Miller
Cover Design: Andrew J. Miller

Printed in the United States of America
10 9 8 7 6 5 4 3 2 1

To Amy,
Love of my life.
And, to my children,
Matthew, Andrew, Bethany, Timothy, Amalia, & Malachi.
And my children-in-law,
Rachel and Sonia

I'd also like to thank a few people for making this book possible. First, my parents, Mabrey and Madge Miller, who taught me first to care, then to care about learning. To Matthew Burch, Life Leadership Ltd. of Pella, Iowa— my friend, we started this journey together as wide-eyed graduate students, thank you for the permission to use the work we did together to inform a new cohort of dreamers. Matthew J. Miller, for the original editing of the manuscript, a task which I would have never undertaken on my own.. Andrew J. Miller, for laying out the book and graphic design: thanks for creative "juice" and great ideas. Drs. Tim Riley, Dale Bertram and Wayne Perry for their review of, and improvements of, my original manuscript. To my colleagues at the Behavioral Pediatric and Family Therapy Program, at Amridge University, and Family Service Association: thanks for your support, encouragement, and tolerance. And, of course to the organizations and businesses who have allowed me to learn my craft – here's hoping they benefited at least as much by my presence.

"Now to him who is able to do exceedingly, abundantly..."

Contents

Running the Practice
    Credentialing

Ethics and Legal Issues

Branding/Marketing
—How Do I Keep Supporting Myself?
    Branding
    Getting Known for What You Do
    Your Unique Selling Point

Marketing

Personality and Marketing

A Naturalistic Approach to Marketing

Now Go Do It!

Introduction

One Therapist's Journey: A Personal History

Circa 1996, working as a master's-prepared therapist with nine years of experience, and having a load of thirty to fifty clients a week, I made the decision to get a doctorate—with the hope of increased opportunities and income. Five years and thousands of dollars later (thank you, honey), PhD in hand, I did have more opportunities opening up, *and the single most important reason for these opportunities—for creating the lifestyle and income I wanted—had very little to do with earning the PhD.*

In fact, it was a specific activity—consulting—that I already had the skills to do (sorry, honey) before I started my doctoral program! It was this unplanned and informal (at least as far as the academic community would see it) experience of working as a consultant—that has given me much greater freedom, control, and income than I had expected. It can do the same for you. That very first project generated a $10,000 contract (quite a windfall for a poor student!) and has led to consulting as a foundational concept on which to build a satisfying career.

How did this happen? As part of my doctoral work, I took a course on qualitative research (using methods not reliant on statistical "number-cruncher" approaches). This spurred my interest in developing skills in research methods in the real world. As part of this interest, a colleague and I approached a family-owned international corporation (annual sales of $500 million) to participate in a research project.

My colleague had an ongoing relationship with the organization as an Employee Assistance provider (EAP) and had developed a relationship with its president. The original idea was to use qualitative methods to improve the corporation's employee satisfaction—a problem my colleague first identified through the EAP referrals. The president accepted the idea, and we began to discuss the research project with the other corporate leadership. However, as we met with senior management to develop the research process, this qualitative research "morphed" into a quite different project.

The corporation had already hired an international survey research company to develop and evaluate the results of an employee satisfaction survey. This outside consultant's process was to develop the survey, obtain the data, run a statistical analysis of the data, and then conduct focus groups to develop action plans to improve employee morale. The corporation leadership asked us, "Can we use your project to follow up on the results of the employee satisfaction survey?" Serendipity and the beginning of a consulting career!

As it turned out, the process of revising the original proposal (based on this change in direction) altered the original focus of our research project. It turned it into a broad consulting contract, and it doubled the cost—read "income" for the consultants!

An event, increasing the scope and revenue generated, that often happens as consulting projects develop. The consultants in this case were charged with designing what the international consultants called the "back end" of the survey process (the focus groups to interpret the results) through sampling three-thousand-plus employees on three shifts in nine plants. We were fortunate that the consultants from the international consultancy corporation were very professional—sharing their data with us, training us on their methods of working with focus groups, and providing their materials to use, which made it a seamless transition and enhanced our effectiveness.

This graduate school project thrust me into the world of consulting. Although my doctoral course work (especially in research) has been helpful to me, nothing that I did in that initial consultation, not any consulting I have done since, has required a doctoral level of knowledge, skills, or competence. The best preparation for working as a consultant has been my work as a therapist combined with a willingness to learn about consulting as a skill set.

Since that "blind start," my knowledge and experience has grown in several ways. As a consultant, I have had the opportunity to teach doctoral and master's courses, provide workshops, actively coach colleagues, and run my own private consulting business that has included working with for-profit companies, nonprofit (mostly behavioral health) agencies and programs, and communities and churches. The result has been less dependence upon a private practice— and the "joys" of dealing with a heavy case load and managed care—or working a "regular job"—a fixed schedule or managing others—and increased my personal freedom while significantly increasing my income. *None of this is out of reach for the average therapist or counselor.* Provided you are willing to learn, work hard, and take careful and necessary risks—such as investing in your own development.

Teaching doctoral students the following concepts and skills has been gratifying. Some have called this the most important course they took in their graduate careers. (I think this was because of the topic, not the teacher—but I continue to nurture a secret hope.) I have watched it free these students from the "helping profession" mindset that limits their opportunities and decreases their earning potential. *This is what this book can do for you.* If it also helps you to significantly increase your income, your confidence in yourself, and reach your preferred lifestyle, well . . . I really like specialty coffees. If you make it really big, I'll hit you up for something more grand later. To get started, let's look at who this book can help.

Who Is This Book For?

This book is written for behavioral health professionals who want to increase their income, government-health-care proof their retirement, avoid the pressure of seeing thirty or more clients a week (and still pay the bills!)—and who want to work in settings where the primary focus is not remedial—providing emotional support or restoring individuals, couples, and families from acute or chronic crisis. In short, this book is for professionals who want to diversify their product lines (this is business language—more on this subject later) or adapt or change their chosen careers in behavioral health.

The focus of this book is on those with a bachelor's or master's degree in a helping profession to teach you to apply the skills you already have to be an effective consultant to organizations and businesses. "Applying the skills you already have" does *not* imply that you won't learn anything new. You will learn how to develop a consultant mindset, identify potential customers, develop proposals and get them funded, and conduct and analyze the work you have done. You will learn about qualitative consulting and how to use basic research skills to make your work effective. You will learn some basic information on managing a consulting business, specific areas of specialty that can be explored, and get a basic understanding of how organizations and businesses think about the people who work for them—their human capital.

When you have completed reading the book, you will be prepared to go out and "get your feet wet" as a consultant— starting you on an exciting, creative, and challenging new path that will increase your own personal control and freedom, and enhance your income. Ready to get started?

But, wait a minute! What about the cynics (like me) out there? Those wary individuals who refuse to be led down some primrose path, who know that the construct "free" always has hidden strings attached, those "late adopters" (as labeled in the technology world) who want a proven track record before purchasing. Let's cut to the bottom line. What will this book *not* teach you? I repeat, *not* teach you? Well, it won't teach you extensive business planning. It won't teach you anything about venture capital. It won't teach you how to launch a major international business.

Rather, this book is focused on the average professional who would like to operate a consulting business as a start-up venture or "add on" to clinical work. This is not designed as a book to "pump you up" and tell you that you can conquer the world. While such books, either realistic or hopeful, might focus on this macro world of extensive business planning, venture capital, and the launch of a national or international big business, this book focuses on a more modest level: helping the average Joe and Jenny begin to get consulting gigs and grow them to whatever size and complexity they desire. The book's aim is to help you put more money in your pocket now, with the skills and experience you already have.

Let me give an example. At the time of writing, I have active consulting contracts with a university, two behavioral health organizations, and two churches. These contracts will add roughly an extra 30 to 45 percent of revenue to my business this year—not too bad for a part-time job (on an average week, no more than five to ten hours). This income is in addition to my "day job" of teaching and running a limited private practice.

Although this level of consulting work will not set the world on fire or lead to a jet-setting lifestyle (extensive travel as a required part of work-life is not my idea of fun anyway), it serves to significantly increase my income, provides security from the ups and downs of private practice (government health care, insurance changes, and snow days, for example), and keeps things interesting. This is one of the great things about consulting—it can be tailored to your interests and the demands of your life.

If you picked up this book with the dream of consulting full-time all over the country—perhaps even internationally— and building a consulting empire, then this book may disappoint you in its modest focus. (Maybe I'll write *that book* when my six kids are all grown and out of the house.) For readers wanting a larger scope, this book will be only one resource to consult. However, if you meet my targeted audience as an average Joe or Jenny, the book is written to prepare you for your first paying job as a consultant, and as a resource to be referred to as your subsequent successes, experience, and scope expand.

So the emphasis here is practical (I come from the Midwest, farm country, and we have little patience for anything else). I aim to teach and equip you to begin to get consulting jobs—now, in your community or region. The end result for some will be a more balanced career and diversified income; for others, this book may mark the beginning of a new and full-time career. It will be particularly useful to anyone with a master's-level or higher counseling degree and may especially resonate with those who share my Marriage and Family Therapy background and a system's focus—although this is definitely not necessary to benefit from the material presented.

Now that we understand one another, let's get right to the point.

For those who want training or resources targeted to either a general professional or mental health specialist, you can find them at www.hsystemsconsulting. com/training.php

CHAPTER 1

Me? A Consultant?

Yes, you. Think about it. Every day, if you are a psychologist, social worker, family therapist, or counselor, you face new clients with new situations and problems that must be resolved. You assess the problems. You design a treatment plan. You implement the planning in coordination with the client. You follow up to make sure the interventions are working. You seek out resources when needed. Many of you present your cases to a supervisor or supervision group, explaining your assessment and interventions.

In addition to these activities, you constantly observe and tweak your own performance. You evaluate your own motives ethically. You struggle with what is best for the individual, the family, and your own business. You deal with the most difficult things in life: clients who are angry, sad, confrontational, potentially violent, or suicidal. Many of your experiences—and the skills that develop in managing them—have prepared you for becoming a consultant.

In fact, your very role is to be consulted. Right now you are consulted by individuals, couples, and families. In the journey of reading this book you will prepare for the leap to larger systems, consulting with work teams, organizations, or businesses. Here is your first hurdle: to see yourself as a professional with valuable experience, knowledge, and skills that transcend the therapy room.

Writing about marriage and family therapists in 1986, Lyman Wynne and colleagues (1984) said: "Because of the systems perspective of family therapy, family therapists can bring special skills to consultation in multiple contexts. At this point in history, we believe that it is timely to sharpen awareness of the rapidly increasing opportunities for consultative roles by family therapists and other systems-oriented health care professionals."

It has been my experience that all of the approaches to behavioral health have similar, yet distinct, advantages that parallel Wynne's comments. The trick is to know your own area of expertise and to capitalize on that advantage.

Among master's-prepared therapists there exists much experience and many skills that can be applied to the area of consulting; yet, most do not provide this as a service. Other than a boom in coaching services, little has been done outside of academia to apply the natural consulting skills of an experienced master's-level therapist to the larger world of consulting with businesses and organizations. This is especially true, in my experience, for those of us trained in Marriage and Family Therapy programs.

One word about coaching—this is a fast-growing area that I will address later in the book, yet I must say here that, in my experience, many who are offering this service have little or no training in the area of general consulting—a deficit this book will address for the reader. Another purpose of writing this book, then, is to build on a general knowledge of consulting and meet the need for a targeted text for behavioral health providers who want to begin consulting or coaching services.

Yes, you already have many skills that can, and do, translate into the world of consulting. As you learn about consulting and the tasks of consulting jobs, begin to visualize how you can apply what you already know and develop a plan to learn what you don't know as you grow into this new line of work.

What Exactly Is a Consultant?
What Does a Consultant Do?

A consultant is one who consults. There, that was easy. I know, I know, you can't use a word to define itself. Consulting itself, however, is such a broad concept that a tight definition can be elusive.

Consulting is providing advice, experience, talents, perspective. Broadly speaking, a consultant is a person who has some influence over another person or system (organization, work team, church) but *without* direct control of the organization or business's operations. Are you saying to yourself, "What?" Well, let me try again.

By contrasting a consultant's role with a management role —a role most people understand—the definition will, I hope, become clear: A manager is a person who *has* the authority to direct people, money, and processes to meet the operational needs of an organization or business. Managers plan, organize, staff, lead, command, and motivate employees to achieve business outcomes. Consultants may also do each of these in running and managing their own business (thus they are managers as well as consultants), but in their roles as consultants they only advise or influence these operations— they do not have direct authority over the decision-making process.

Consulting, itself, is often more of a process than a fixed commodity. There are skills and tasks common to all consultants (contracting, proposal writing, billing) and ones that are unique to any given consultant (creating an IT network geared toward a creative mindset, or using your unique social network to find new funding sources, for example). It is the uniqueness of these tasks that makes defining consulting so difficult. However, if you master the consulting process—its tasks and skill set—while gaining an understanding of the field, you will be positioned to maximize your own unique experience, education, and skills to be an advisor, problem solver, or coach as your interests and ability lead you. If this is a difficult stretch for you, then you might consider hiring your own consultant coach to aid in your own development and success. (Mondays and Tuesdays over coffee tend to work best for me.) Despite my joking, I am serious—working with a coach is a great way to jump start your learning and success.

Reasons for Expanding Your Revenue Stream Through Consulting

Why consulting? There are several reasons to consider this as a new revenue stream for your business. First, the helping professions are under attack. Providers of behavioral health services are likely to be increasingly operating in a competitive market that is rigidly narrow in focus, requiring increasing amounts of paperwork, longer hours, and producing a lower income. At worst, the helping professions may evolve into a pseudo-governmental function where the services and income are limited to "approved levels" dictated by the government and insurance companies. Treatment methods may be subjected to governmental-approved approaches and conditions, forcing therapists into a focus on triage and referral or narrowing their scope of practice.

Sears and colleagues, writing in the preface to *Consultation Skills for Mental Health Professionals* in 2006 gave the following warning: "The field of mental health is changing. With nationwide budget cuts, community mental health centers and other agencies are cutting back on the number of high-level mental health providers they employ. Aside from the positive aspects of doing consultation work, consulting may become a necessity for many clinicians to provide the means to make a decent living."

Note that this was written *before* the passage of a national health care bill, the subsequent news of rationed care in nations such as England, and news about rural physicians' limiting services (such as the whooping cough vaccine) due to reimbursement rates so low that they lose money to provide them, and recent decisions by insurance companies such as dropping policies covering individual children or eliminating health care coverage entirely. But we'll save the political lessons for a different book.

IIIIIIIIIIIIIIIIII

In America, providers of behavioral health services in private practice are already fighting this limiting of services with increasing regularity. My private practice, part of a pediatric group that has providers who specialize in treating toileting issues, recently decided not to see clients from a particular government payer. Why? Because they refuse to pay for sessions with the parents without the child present. Sometimes a separate session is necessary, in our view, when parents are responsible for implementing the treatment protocols with children with behavioral problems. Furthermore, their rule applies even if the child is under age five! Thus, we simply informed this third-party payer that this decision forces us into either providing inadequate care (an ethical violation), changing the focus of what we treat, or reducing our ability to stay in business (providing multiple hours of pro-bono services weekly). As a result we no longer see those clients.

||||||||||||||||||

On the national level, government has recently turned toward a higher level of participation in the private sector in the automotive and banking systems. Health care will be changing dramatically. If the profession loses even a couple of these battles each year, then the change will come in the not-too-distant future. Now, how does being a consultant sound? I thought so too. Let's move on.

Consulting is a broad and diverse field that allows you to pick and choose what you do based on your interests. I have had students coming out of many different backgrounds who were able to use their experiences to develop contracts with larger organizations. For example

◊ A second-career student (formerly an accountant) focused on helping accounting teams.

◊ A pastor's wife worked to improve church organization and functioning.

◊ A real estate professional used consulting approaches to develop new funding streams.

◊ A career military man began to look for opportunities post-enlistment for consulting.

◊ A second-generation daughter in a family-based business focused on family functioning in family-based businesses.

All of these individuals were well positioned to use their unique life experiences to develop a niche for consulting. You can do the same.

CHAPTER 2

Developing the Right Mindset

Limitations of the Therapist/Counselor Mindset

Having worked in the world of the helping professions for more than twenty years, I have noticed a typical blind spot for many in the field. If you find that the following does not describe you, consider yourself fortunate—you are a step ahead!

Many helping professionals in my experience have a basic or learned paradigm of a "service" or "ministry" mindset. This makes it difficult for these individuals to ask for or even demand appropriate payment and benefits for the services they provide. This attitude is further reinforced by the economic environment in which they operate.

Recently, I heard of an undergraduate student (no degree yet) with an internship in accounting being paid $15 an hour. How does that compare with the counseling world? Try a year or more internship with a small or no stipend—read "no pay"—even after earning a master's or a doctoral degree. Financial parity has certainly not reached the counseling world.

Thus reinforced as to their lack of intrinsic value, the attitude of many professionals seems to be that one must adopt an altruistic mentality to add value to this inequity. The services provided by therapists, then, are somehow tainted if we openly admit that we are participating in a business. A business, the very nature of which is viewed by some as existing only to perpetuate itself or make a profit, is thus viewed as being of less value than, and in contrast with, the altruistic helper mindset. This generalization does not describe everyone in the field, however, and those holding this view often conflict with those who are comfortable seeing human services as a business.

You can find information on therapist and consultant incomes and pay calculators at www.hsystemsconsulting. com/therapist-pay.php

The discomfort between those who want the organization to be financially successful and those who provide the services often causes a split in our thinking. As in many management-labor environments, we engage in a we-they dichotomy, often creating caricatures of people on the other side, projecting judgment on them much like Dr. Seuss illustrated with the "Star-bellied Sneetches" who disdained and worked against those who "have none upon thars."

Laborers eye management with distrust as those who are only interested in the bottom line, while managers view the workers as unreliable and untrustworthy, as "bleeding hearts" who have no appreciation for the realities of making a business survive and thrive. This affliction is particularly virulent among young therapists, whom time and experience usually temper—although it can persist with those who are not so young.

To be successful as a human systems consultant, you must get beyond the black-and-white thinking that you must choose to *either* be oriented toward service *or* profit. Again, if you have already made this shift or were never afflicted with this attitude, congratulations—you are ahead of the game. The rest of you, read on.

The false dichotomy mentioned above can be maintained only if you work for someone else—be that government, nonprofits, or a for-profit venture. The self-employed quickly understand the relationship between service and profit. Service cannot be given away (at least not in great quantity) without the business suffering and eventually failing. Likewise, poor service, especially combined with high costs (poor value) will eventually damage or kill the business, unless perhaps the company has cornered the market—and even then they are storing up resentment for when a competitor arises.

Understand, those of you who are still uncomfortable with a profit mindset, that for-profit businesses do provide pro-bono work or write off bad debt for those who cannot afford the provided services, but this cannot be the typical business practice, or the business fails.

Helping professionals must transition out of this mindset to be successful as consultants. This does not mean that the consultant must be a "hard sell" personality. In fact, many successful consultants are not the sales type at all. Many prefer and operate as relationship builders, a trait most therapists are skilled and experienced in from their daily work, and a profitable business allows one to provide pro-bono work when needed with a peaceful and joyful heart—not fearful of failing or full of resentment.

One of the first tasks in moving from the world of therapy to consulting—and one that will continue as long as you work as a consultant—is confronting your internal barriers. Adlerians call this your private fiction. Cognitive therapists refer to this as cognitive distortions. Postmodern therapists call it the problem-saturated story.

Aaron Beck (1979) proposed, and Jeffrey Young (1999) expanded upon the idea of an Early Maladaptive Schema (EMS) that acts as a cognitive "structure for screening, coding, and evaluation the stimuli that impinge on the organism. ...On the basis [of which] the individual is able to orient himself... and to categorize and interpret experiences." In other words, it is often the cognitive picture we have of ourselves and the world (schema) that influences our interpretation of events.

In the counseling world we often call this "baggage" that each of us carries with us from our earlier experiences. Examples include the bright and successful student who fears that the next semester will be *the* semester where he fails; the millionaire who continues to question whether she has done enough to be a success; and the teacher who adamantly argues that as a superior teacher he deserves more latitude than other teachers, and ignores the impact of his grandiosity. These are all examples of Early Maladaptive Schemas being acted out.

The following list is my adaptation of Beck and Young's Early Maladaptive Schemas revised to focus on possible emotional/mental roadblocks for the new business consultant. These items, to the degree they accurately represent the average beginning consultant, may shed some light on possible pitfalls.

Cognitive/behavioral/emotional baggage that consultants may need to confront

1. Fears about Disruptions in their Relationships or Rejection by Others
   a. Loss of support (including emotional), protection, or connection with family, colleagues, business associates, or clients
   b. Fears about being taken advantage of or hurt by competitors, clients, or partners
   c. Fears of inferiority in skills, knowledge, or intellect
   d. Fears of social isolation

2. Fears about Autonomy and Performance
   a. Pressure to be over-reliant on others or the failure to allow oneself to rely on others when appropriate
   b. Perceived personal vulnerability or fear of failure

c.   Over-involvement emotionally with a significant other

3.   Challenges to Emotional Boundaries and Limits
       a.   Over-confidence in one's rights and abilities
       b.   Poor frustration tolerance and self-control

4.   Challenges to Interpersonal Relating
       a.   Heightened need to please others
       b.   Excessive need to avoid conflict
       c.   Overly focused on attention-seeking or recognition

5.   Over-vigilance/Inhibition
       a.   Pessimism—seeing disaster around every corner
       b.   Emotional inhibition
       c.   Unrelenting standards/hyper-criticalness
       d.   Hyper-punitiveness

What baggage do you bring to the work of being a consultant? Are you worried about how you will negotiate your current and future relationships? Wondering if you can operate on your own and perform adequately? Do you fear (secretly or overtly) your own self-control? Believe you'll get "sucked in" too deeply to others' conflicts, needs, or demands? Feel compelled to see a doom and gloom future? These fears must be recognized and countered. You will resolve them only by taking the risk of facing them (in small achievable steps) and successfully overcoming them. In therapy, it is basic exposure—but here we must intervene for ourselves. If it is too difficult to face these fears on your own, then hiring a qualified coach to assist in this process may be beneficial.

Another barrier is transcending the mindset of therapy. In consulting projects a trained therapist may note behavior that is "of psychological interest" that needs to be ignored. As a consultant this knowledge can be valuable, but the reason that you have been hired is for a business, rather than a mental health need. It can be tempting to fall back into focusing on good boundaries, addressing mental health problems, or confronting problematic behavior, but this should be done only if it addresses the goals of the consultation. In his discussion about creating a Council of Advisors for a family-based business, Fleming (2000) wrote: "Since a critical tenet of this book is that family baggage is usually what kills family businesses, it may seem strange that psychologists are listed as only ancillary members of the Council of Advisors. That's because there's always the danger that the psychologist will want to play therapist. The knowledge of psychology is needed, but not the application of therapy."

‖‖‖‖‖‖‖‖‖‖‖‖‖‖‖

A word about education and consulting: You do not need a PhD in order to be a consultant. While a PhD certainly helps (particularly in the area of applying research methods), having real-world experiences, first as a therapist and second with businesses, along with a willingness to learn, are far more important. Some business people even consider a PhD a liability. Those business leaders refer to PhDs as "egg heads" and assume that coming from the ivory tower of academia means they have little practical knowledge or experience in the "real world" of business.

||||||||||||||||||||

Thus, a successful shift into being a consultant requires a departure from the limitations of the therapist mindset—but certainly not abandoning the skill set and experience gained as a therapist. Now we will turn to examining the mindset of a successful consultant.

Shifts in Developing a Consultant Mindset

What makes a good consultant? I believe that one of the most important things for human systems consultants is to recognize the unique traits of your personality, training, and experience and how that sets you apart from the average consultant. This specialization points the way to your strengths, as well as areas of needed growth. Note that focusing on these traits may result in recognizing gaps in your preparation—areas where you may need to gain skills or experience. If you read this book thoughtfully, you will also identify some of these gaps. Recognizing areas for growth should not stop you—rather, this recognition should be used to develop a plan of attack for how you will get the necessary skills or experience.

Characteristics of a Consultant

Peter Block, in his book *Flawless Consulting,* boils down the characteristics a consultant must possess to two: being authentic and attending to the steps of the consulting process (technical, interpersonal, and consulting). In many ways this is sufficient. Be authentic and learn how to do consulting. In fact, this book is built somewhat on a similar philosophy—if you can build trusting relationships and learn how to complete the tasks of consulting then voila! You are a consultant! However, as you may want an idea of the traits that make a good consultant, let's look at some of the recognized traits that are beneficial.

Here are some terms collected from the literature that have been said to describe the necessary traits of a consultant:

◊ Focused

◊ Detail-oriented

◊ Tenacious

◊ Enterprising

◊ Visionary

◊ Confident

◊ Bold

◊ Self-initiating

◊ Resilient

◊ Action-oriented

◊ Intuitive

◊ People-focused

◊ Independent

◊ Flexible

◊ Committed

◊ Challenging

◊ Innovative

◊ Assertive

◊ Insightful

◊ Communicative

◊ Positive

◊ Meticulous

And this is only a sampling. I can't predict how this list will make you feel, but I suspect that it probably is overwhelming to many. Is this "the consultant as Superman or Wonder Woman?" See them perform astounding feats! There is no one like them! Wow. It doesn't fit with my—admittedly cynical—view of the world.

What happened to being authentic? Do you know anyone who possesses all these traits? I don't. And I suspect you don't either. If you think you do, I would ask you, "Just how well do you know this person?" If you believe that you are that person, then take a moment to look up the term *narcissist*.

For the rest of us (some of whom admittedly may go too far the other direction, wondering in our low self-esteem,

"Who would ever hire me?"), let's get down to brass tacks, as they say. What is *really* important in succeeding as a consultant? Here's my take on the subject. First, the old authenticity/trustworthiness/integrity/character—whatever you want to call it—I believe is critical to long-term success. Do you want to work with people you don't trust, whom you don't believe will be honest and professional? Done well, consulting is a relationship business, and if you do not value these relationships and engender trust with your clients, you may not be a consultant very long.

Second, relationship skills. Not only do you need to be authentic with clients, you also need a certain amount of ability to work well with people. Again, the consulting we are focusing on is a people-centered career, not simply work as a technical specialist. You must be able to market, build relationships, and understand human dynamics and individual psychology at least to some degree. You also need to be assertive, to deal with emotionally charged situations and clients—the tougher side of relationship skills.

Third, an ability to understand larger systems. At first, this may be threatening. How do you learn to understand larger systems? The same way we learn other skills: education, experience, observation. Congratulations. You have already begun. By choosing to read this book, you are already on your way, as we explore managerial models of human capital, and as you read the case studies. Working as a consultant puts you in a world where there are multiple layers: contradictory demands, wants, and needs; unclear, non-verbal, mixed communication; a zero-sum win/lose environment operating as collaboration and "family." Skills in understanding how businesses function, what rocks hide under the calm surface, and how the ripples of a stone cast into that pond may reverberate throughout the system is important.

Fourth, the ability to complete consulting tasks. That is the primary purpose for writing this book: to help you learn the tasks of consulting. How do you get clients, develop conceptual agreement, complete a proposal, price the job, bill for your services, develop management reports—all tasks the consultant must master. These skills open up the possibility of your having more control over your work life and increasing your income, but you must master the skills and tasks to succeed.

Fifth, flexibility. I hesitated to include this one. What profession doesn't benefit from flexibility? Probably few if any. Nevertheless, I believe it is an important trait to note in consulting. Leaders and businesses operate in a dynamic environment. People, the primary medium of our brand of consulting, are malleable and variable. As a consultant, you will experience surprises, bends in the road, hidden agendas, and change as part of the landscape, and you must be able to adapt, often on the fly. Incidentally, just in case you haven't already noticed this in your work, being a therapist is good training for developing this trait.

Sixth, business skills. To be a consultant means running a business—even if that business has only one employee, you. You must be able to organize yourself. To set goals. Engage and work with other professionals (accountants, lawyers, and others). Market, manage, and plan. All the tasks of any type of business become part of your daily work.

That's pretty much it. Sure, it's nice to be brilliant, creative, and visionary, but thankfully, it's typically not necessary, and for most of us these traits may be an event—born out of experience, a different vantage point, or luck—rather than a steady and dependable trait. Good news! The same can be said for most of the clients you will serve (my apologies to all my past and present clients). If they were consistently brilliant, creative, and visionary, then they probably wouldn't need your services anyway—see the narcissist comment above. Now let's take a look into the "new world" into which you will be moving—the world of business.

You can take an online assessment of your readiness as a consultant on the HSC website: www.hsystemsconsulting. com/resources.php

CHAPTER 3

The World of Business and Consulting

B usiness runs on taking care of the bottom line. Making a profit is what a business exists to achieve. Even "nonprofits" and governmental programs are judged based on the size of their budgets or the amount of services they provide. The consultant must never forget this. That is not to say that there are no organizations that act in a caring manner toward people—many do—it is just that the reason businesses exist is to perpetuate themselves and grow. Without profit the business ceases to exist, and its services or products are no longer provided to its customers.

Businesses must maintain a tenuous balance: keeping an unwavering focus on improving the bottom line while prudently managing the company's resources (the single largest dollar-wise item being human capital). Gersick and colleagues note that in a ten-year period, 90 percent of entrepreneurial ventures fail. Bloomberg Businessweek

(2002) reportedthat in a thirteen-year period, 33 percent of the *Fortune 500* firms had disappeared. The article went on to estimate that the average lifespan for a *Fortune 500* company is forty to fifty years.

Many top administrators understand that people are a vital part, and often the most important part, of the success or failure of organizations, and in my experience many even have a sincere desire to treat their employees well. In fact, I've seen that conversations about the importance of the employees are often *initiated* by these top executives. Often this is in direct contradiction to the beliefs of direct-line employees about upper management (which is a trust issue and may be the focus of a consultation project itself). Among employees, the belief may be that upper managers only care about maximizing their own profit.

One of the difficulties I have noticed with young professionals in the behavioral health field is a reluctance to see their own work as engaging in a *business practice*. This shows up in several ways. Many are uncomfortable with marketing their services or skills. Some maintain a black-and-white thinking that professionals are either in the field for the "right reasons" or just in it for the money. Many have trouble collecting fees, determining a proper value for their services, or setting up their own activities as a proper business venture. These hurdles in thinking must be met and overcome.

A Brief (I Promise) History of Therapists as Consultants

Family Therapy/Systems Consultation

Although consultation to organizations undoubtedly has been around for as long as people have organized themselves, the application of a family therapy framework, beginning with its initial systemic focus, to these organizations is relatively new. Marriage and Family Therapy (MFT) began in the 1950s when some theorists began to develop a strong interest in machine "systems" (von Bertalanffy, 1968) and how that systems theory could be applied to human systems, specifically to their work with families (Bateson, 1972). The field of MFT embraced this systemic view eagerly and began to focus on the nuclear family as a system of roles, functions, communication, and behavior.

Over time this interest broadened into looking at larger family systems (kinship networks and extended families) with the work of Intergenerational, Multiple Systems Therapy, and Network Therapy approaches. In time, it was natural that this model would be used to assess, explain, and intervene in non-family systems as well. This focus on larger systems ultimately found voice in the publication in the 1980s of Wynne and colleagues' *Systems Consultation*, and the development of new approaches such as Medical MFT and Coaching.

What has failed to develop is a coordinated, informed approach to systems consultation as a general practice, despite some early attempts, notably by Capelle (1979) and

Boverie (1991). The common approach has been to apply MFT skills and models directly to working with organizations rather than to incorporate the knowledge and language of either consulting or business (see McDowell, 1999; Fetsch & Zimmerman, 1999, for examples).

Since that early adoption of a systemic view of human relationships, the MFT field has moved away from its systemic roots into postmodern approaches to therapy. (I was fortunate to experience both "waves" of therapeutic frameworks in my formal training, and as a consultant I especially value my systemic training in understanding and working in larger systems.)

At about the same time that MFT was leaving its systemic framework, businesses began to pay *more* attention to systemic approaches and theory. Peter Senge, coming out of MIT, published *The Fifth Discipline* (1990), which postulated that the highest order of business functioning is to adopt an informed systems view of itself. So as MFT was moving away from a systems paradigm, businesses were focusing more on their interconnectedness and adopting that same framework.

Modern approaches to manufacturing such as Kaizen, Six Sigma, Lean, Just-in-Time (Vollmann, et al., 2004) and others have focused on understanding how systems operated best—including human systems. Business practices in other sectors have shared similar interests.

Meanwhile, theoretically speaking, MFT marched on, leaving behind the corpse of its systemic past. However, even when it was in its prime and attention was focused intently through a systemic lens, much of the MFT literature, which focused on consulting to larger systems, failed to transcend a therapeutic framework. Literature that uses the language of therapy (assessment, intervention), ignores business issues (the bottom line, budgets), and ignores the business of consulting (proposal writing, contracting)—thus giving the impression that applying therapeutic experience and skills to larger systems is a simple, easy, and natural transition that can occur almost overnight.

Furthermore, the application of postmodern approaches to consulting is lacking in the MFT literature and is largely ignored in the business consulting literature. MFTs and other health professionals (organizational psychologists perhaps may be excepted) who want to consult with larger systems are often left to a trial-and-error approach, or are forced to translate the literature of the business world into their professional language if they want to become systems consultants.

Thus, there exists a naive view, adopted by some, that a knowledge of a theoretical framework, here systems theory, and human relationship experience is sufficient to work with larger systems. But consulting with larger organizations as a human systems professional requires knowledge and skills in all three of the following areas: human behavior, business operations, and the consulting profession. Wynne et al. developed a continuum of MFT roles that in its pictorial model placed systems consultation at the center of the continuums of therapy—administration and supervision—teaching (Wynne et al. 1986), which certainly reflects the complexity of knowledge and skills required as a consultant.

The good news is this: Many of the constructs, metaphors, and skills that are learned in becoming and practicing as a therapist, particularly in the application of systems theory, can translate to the business world. Think of your own work history. What memories do ideas such as homeostasis, triangulation, boundaries, enmeshment, or disengagement bring up? From a postmodern stance you might focus on problem-saturated stories, externalization, and deconstructing those stories. If you are well versed in these theories, it is not difficult to see how these issues affect organizations and the individuals within them as well.

The ideas, models, and assessment tools you learned in your professional training will continue to help you in your work as a consultant; however, a warning is justified here. (Cue lightning strike and roll of thunder!) A failure to adapt to the business context—learning the literature, language, and applications of businesses—may limit your utility, perceived expertise, or revenue. Remember not to stay stuck in the therapist's language or mindset as you begin to interact with business people. (In old systems terminology, this would be akin to being rigidly inflexible—a bad quality for families, and presumably, consultants as well.) MFT terminology like "equifinality or rapport" may be common ideas to therapists, but businesses have a professional language of their own, and if you do not speak it, you must educate your clients to the language of therapy—a more difficult task, which requires more commitment from the client to be successful.

Despite these challenges, many authors writing about consulting see training as a family therapist as critical to working within certain business environments—notably in consultation with human service organizations and family-based businesses (Gordon & Nicholson, 2008). Still others—such as Fleming (2000), who recommended having a psychologist as an ancillary member of the Council of Advisors for family-based businesses—identify the importance of consultation with experts in human behavior in these environments. In these niches, and perhaps in others, an understanding of family systems—or more broadly, human systems—may give the consultant a distinct advantage.

Industrial/Organizational Consulting

Many psychologists provide consulting on some level. This may be clinical, coaching, recruitment, dealing with troubled employees, or some higher-level measurement and intervention into business systems. Although this text is *not* focused on industrial-organizational consulting (I/O), a concise field within psychology that has a literature of its own, the overlap in some areas is undeniable. New consultants will certainly benefit from learning from this specialized literature and may interact with I/O psychologists in their work as a consultant.

Therefore, we will benefit from a brief review of this field's development over time and its impact on consulting. At the same time, we will attempt to identify the strengths and weaknesses of such an approach, not to denigrate organizational consulting—far from it, I hope—but to help you understand when a consulting problem is best approached from this stance versus a human systems approach.

Industrial-organizational psychology developed out of academic work in the early twentieth century, by Hugo Munsterberg (1913) and Fredrick W. Taylor (1911) and others, and its subsequent application during World War I to the need for classifying individuals and assigning troops quickly.

In 1917, the *Journal of Applied Psychology* began to be published, and it became an important coalescing influence in the field. In the 1920s doctoral degrees began to be offered, which specialized in industrial psychology. Later, after the importance of social factors in the workplace was recognized based on Mayo's Hawthorne studies (discussed later in the book), the field expanded to work with many different industries and organizations.

Use of the scientific method and research tools (both qualitative and quantitative) has been the hallmark of the tools of I/O consulting. I/O methods and measures have been applied to many areas in business including, but not limited to, employee selection, performance appraisals, team effectiveness, and work processes, among many others.

The field reached maturity with the establishment of Division 14 of the American Psychological Association in 1946 and later its incorporation as the Society for Industrial and Organizational Psychology in 1983. I/O psychologists now provide consulting activities within multiple formats as both internal consultants and external entrepreneurs. This profession continues to contribute much in the application of psychological theory, constructs, and research skills to organizations and businesses. The MFT consultant would do well not to ignore this literature, as it comes out of a rich and diverse heritage and can offer paradigms, theory, and tools that may be beneficial.

CHAPTER 4

The Therapist's Tool Bag—Natural Strengths as a Consultant

Knowledge and Skills that May Transfer to Consulting

At this point you may be wondering, "Is this worth it?" Do I have to start all over, learn a new field of expertise? Do I have what it takes to be a consultant? Let me reassure you once more—much of the skills, knowledge, and expertise gained through being a therapist prepare you well for being a consultant. First of all, consulting is about people—unless you can dream up a scenario where the consultant is so highly technical in his or her focus (IT or accounting come closest perhaps) that no contact with the human side of the business is necessary. And even then I would question it! Ever know any "techies" that didn't seem to relate to humans? Did it impact their effectiveness? In my experience interpersonal skills are inescapable in business. As a therapist—just by your type, your training, your knowledge and experience with people—you already have a set of skills and understanding that will stand you in good stead as a consultant.

Natural Fits
for the Therapist/Counselor Consultant

The following areas are what most seasoned clinicians do as a "consultant"—that is, operating at a meta-level within their natural skill set and field. This provides some easy and natural ways to begin to develop an entrepreneurial mindset and experience.

Many, however, never reach beyond this framework. This intra-field consulting is fine, and it often works well to supplement the clinical work of seeing clients. If that is your focus and such opportunities present themselves, then all is well and good. However, *this book is focused on helping you reach beyond that framework* to a broader definition of yourself as a human systems consultant—a specialist not tied to a particular field but with a skill set applicable to a larger context of humans involved in businesses or organizations.

This section is presented to help ease you into seeing consulting as a natural step in your development as a professional. I also hope that it will help you to see these opportunities either as an intentional area of focus (specializing in these activities) or as a preparatory stage for work as a human systems consultant to organizations or businesses.

Supervision

Many mental health professionals get their start in consulting by providing some level of supervision of other professionals within their field. For many, this is a promotion or a change in duties as a part of their employment. Eventually these experts often get drawn into expanding their roles into mental health consultation, behavioral consultation, program consultation, or community consultation that becomes the first departure into an "organizational" framework (Sears, et al., 2006).

For me, the supervision role happened almost immediately, in less than one year after finding full-time employment! In nine months I moved from the role of a "therapist" to a "program coordinator" and took on the role of providing day-to-day management functions over a group of peer therapists—a move that required a fast transition in job functions and a significant shift in roles.

For most this may come by moving into a management position and providing day-to-day supervision. For others, the shift to a role as supervisor may be a task that they provide for an organization as part of its staff, and then, later having made a shift to a private practice, becoming a contracted employee. As experience and education progress, the therapist may become a clinical supervisor—listening to case presentations, providing education to therapy staff, and taking on the accountability of overseeing the therapeutic work of a group of therapists.

While this is not traditionally thought of under the title of "consultation," many of the skills and activities of supervision translate to the tasks of working as a consultant—running meetings, the role of being the "expert," group dynamics, and many other aspects will be similar. MSW and doctoral-level professionals may especially fall into this track. This role may also be expanded by providing supervision toward the initial licensure for other professionals, an activity that for some has provided an additional revenue stream.

There are many resources on supervision, and providing quality supervision is certainly a specialty area that requires it own set of knowledge, skills, and experience. These attributes are likely achieved by completing advanced coursework, going through a training process, or having hands-on experiences. My purpose here is not to prepare you for becoming a clinical supervisor, a task outside the scope of this book. But please note that if you have this experience or training, you are well on your way to understanding and developing many of the skills of being a consultant.

Psychoeducation

The first, and often only, experience many therapists have with consultation is through contracting to provide psychoeducation services. As therapists gain recognition for their work, develop a network of trusted referral sources, and engage in working with professionals from multiple settings—educational, ecclesiastical, governmental, medical—they often are asked, or motivated, to provide some type of educational activity. This may be engaged in to maintain or develop a good referral source, out of a passion to teach, gain referrals, or other motivations. Frequently the earliest activities are provided at low cost or no cost as therapists develop their careers and establish their brand. In time—as their networks, reputations, and referral bases grow—these activities are likely to be seen as less attractive, unnecessary, or even a burden, and many cease to provide these services, focusing on their clinical work.

If your plan is to use workshops, speeches, and teaching as a way to develop your business with the plan of eventually transitioning out of these activities—no problem (just make sure you continue to have some type of marketing plan). But most therapists do not follow a rigorous business plan, and abandoning this course is often simply by default.

Psychoeducation services can themselves be a revenue stream for some consultants. If you enjoy preparing and presenting psychoeducational materials, get excited about live performance, and are willing to market, plan, and carry out such educational endeavors, then this might be a good product line for you. Contracting with businesses, organizations, churches, civic groups, self-help organizations, and other entities to provide psychoeducation services is regular fare for some in the field. There are many resources available online or through your local bookstore for learning how to market, present, and profit from these sources if this is of interest to you.

Less Natural (But Still Very Possible!) Fits as a Consultant

One of my conclusions, based on reviews of the current literature, is that many in the fields of social work, counseling, and Marriage and Family Therapy have focused on the previously listed natural fits for consultation. In fact, much of the early literature on consulting with organizations in these fields places an emphasis on applying therapy principles to organizations as I have noted. These approaches fail to acknowledge that business has its own language, processes, practices, paradigms, and resources.

Today businesses expect consultants to understand business—not necessarily to be experts in the operation of business themselves, but rather to be experts in their own tradition with a good general understanding of business. *Businesses may be reluctant to engage therapists as consultants if they do not have this business knowledge.* Many businesses are by nature "expert shy." In fact, some experts have recommended that consultants with a PhD should *not* list their doctorate, for fear that this would make businesses reject them as "egg heads" with little or no common sense and business savvy.

Team Building

In my observation of our profession, team building activities or addressing problems in a work team may be the first non-therapeutic consulting that the professional experiences. The consultant's activities may be limited to something such as administering a personality test (the Myers-Briggs Type Indicator has been used widely for this) and then providing some activity to help the team air complaints, communicate, or problem solve. At other times it may be to apply some recreational activity (such as offered by recreational therapists) as part of a team retreat or strategic planning session. Many resources, such as Scannell's *Games Trainers Play* (1986), focus on helping consultants provide activities for team building or similar events.

Contracting for team building may be a simple agreement, for instance a fixed- fee contract, which pays the consultant based on his or her time or completion of the project. At this early stage, the consultant is typically "flying by the seat of the pants" in applying an approach, tools, or interventions. Much of the approach and content is likely to come directly from education, rather than from experience or original research.

Organization Collaboration

On a higher level, but very similar to the idea of "teamwork," a consultant can help whole organizations learn to work and play together. I once worked as the director of a project (Children and Families Strengthened Through an Array of Services or "CF STAR"—how's that for a mouthful?) to integrate the behavioral health services of four large providers in one city. This project led to a number of improvements including these:

◊ A shared intake and referral process to provide a
   single point of access for clients

◊ Shared staff supervision, hiring, training, and program development

◊ The joint hiring of a psychiatrist to provide services in each organization

◊ Purchase, development, and implementation of a shared clinical record/billing software package

◊ The securing of over $3.5 million for the organizations in local funding to integrate, supervise, and implement joint services

Although I was technically an employee of one of the four agencies (insurance issue), I answered to all four senior executives and operated on a day-to-day basis much like a consultant in my role as director with each of the four organizations. This type of integration rarely occurs without strong, and often independent, leadership—a role that may be accomplished best by the right external or internal consultant.

Many nonprofit organizations that want to gain access to grant funding may need to collaborate with other organizations, educational or community groups, which provides an opportunity for grant writing, facilitation services, or coordination and management skills (this is one way your business grows building on your earlier contacts—I continue to write grants for one of the CF STAR organizations eight years after leaving the director position) that can easily be provided by an outside consultant with this expertise.

Strategic Planning

Do you like planning, structure, and logical analysis? Perhaps consulting with organizations to develop their strategic plan will be a niche you choose. Many organizations have adopted the strategic plan as a primary format for driving the future of their organization and often employ an outside "mediator" or "strategic planner" to assist them. There is well-documented literature, multiple frameworks and tools, and colleagues with experience to mentor you. If this is an interest, it could become a part-time or full-time product line.

Leadership Development

Another potential niche is in the area of leadership development. While similar to, and perhaps overlapping with, coaching or training, leadership development has become a specialized area of its own. With awareness growing for the need for developing and retaining good leadership, this could also be a profitable niche. Again, like strategic planning there is well-developed literature in this field. (For a basic review of leadership theory, see Sears et al., 2006)

Appreciative Inquiry

A recent approach to working with organizations and businesses that has a therapeutic "feel" is the Appreciative Inquiry (AI) movement. What is Appreciative Inquiry? The Appreciative Inquiry Commons, a self-described "worldwide portal" for academic resources and practical tools describes it as follows:

Appreciative Inquiry is about the coevolutionary search for the best in people, their organizations, and the relevant world around them. In its broadest focus, it involves systematic discovery of what gives "life" to a living system when it is most alive, most effective, and most constructively capable in economic, ecological, and human terms. AI involves, in a central way, the art and practice of asking questions that strengthen a system's capacity to apprehend, anticipate, and heighten positive potential.

AI is a way of asking questions that focuses on the strengths of individuals and organizations and assists them in strengthening the system and creating positive change. As a consultant, adopting an AI focus can identify you as a particular brand of consultant that may be attractive to organizations familiar with or seeking this strength-based approach. The ideas, skills, and tools used in AI work are also easily transferrable to other consulting work and as such are valuable to any consultant. A review of the theory and practice of AI is however beyond the scope of this book, and readers who wish to pursue this may consult the resources at the end as a starting point for learning more about AI.

Coaching

Coaching is a sub-set of consulting and may be used as a strategy within a consulting process or as a stand-alone service. Within a consulting process it is likely to be an intervention that addresses some perceived deficit or need in a particular employee, manager, or leader (Flaherty, 1999).

As a stand-alone service it may be focused on a range of issues, from job performance to life satisfaction.

Many mental health professionals have begun to offer coaching services as a product; however, in my experience their qualifications to provide these services often remain a mystery. Have they worked as a senior executive in a business or organization outside their own counseling practice? Did their training include some coursework on consulting, coaching, or leadership? Or have they simply attended a workshop and created a new product line? I fear it often is the latter of these scenarios.

Coaching, as opposed to a mental health service, is focused on meeting a business need: career development, work-life balance, or job performance. While these have some overlap with counseling, and having the training and knowledge of a counselor is valuable here, you cannot forget that the basic focus is different. In addition, the leader may expect a higher level of understanding of business practices from a coach than from a therapist.

The overlap between what I will call a pure business consultation (without coaching) and coaching as a stand-alone service occurs in many areas: marketing, proposal development, and even the services or interventions may be the same, but coaching as an independent product has some particular challenges and opportunities that I will address here.

According to Kempa and White (2002) modern coaching has existed in some form since the 1940s. Other writers point out that advisors or personal coaching relationships have existed throughout history and point to examples such as the Oracle at Delphi, Aristotle, Machiavelli, and Cardinal Richelieu.

Certainly there has always been a need at the leadership level for an outside advisor role. At whatever point you draw the starting line for coaching as a profession, it is still true that after all that history there still is no single consensually validated definition for what coaching "is." It is no surprise, then, that its effectiveness is similarly more assumptive than proven at this point. In Kempa and White's review of the literature the authors claimed that there were only five empirical studies on the efficacy of coaching. They concluded that there is "modest evidence" that coaching works for job performance, productivity, self-awareness and development, and leadership effectiveness.

Despite the dearth of empirical attention, McGovern (2001) found that 86 percent of executives report coaching as "beneficial" and reports the following statistics:

◊ 51 percent of coached executives reported increased productivity

◊ 48 percent reported increased work quality

◊ 77 percent improved their relationships with direct reports

◊ 71 percent improved their relationships with key stakeholders

◊ 67 percent reported improved teamwork

◊ 63 percent indicated an improvement in their relationships with peers

◊ 93 percent would recommend the coaching to others

The authors then calculated the return on investment (ROI), which compares the cost of the coaching to its benefit to the company, and determined it to be 5.7 times the investment.

Going back to the 1980s, Lukaszewski (1988) noted certain emerging traits of executive environments that argue for the need of executive coaching. Specifically, he observed that senior managers are becoming more isolated, businesses are in a higher state of change, employees move around more, organizations are becoming multicultural environments, and executives rarely receive behavioral feedback. If you have ever been a senior manager, or the friend of one, you will undoubtedly understand the isolation that occurs in a position with no peers in the organization, a need to work with those who report directly to you, and a board that manages with minimal involvement in the day-to-day activities of the business.

What is executive coaching? A partnership to help the leader resolve a business dilemma, recognize and resolve a "tragic flaw," or grow and improve. Generally, the focus is specifically on the leader, which often is different than general consulting work. The coaching is for his or her benefit as a leader in the organization or company. However, good coaches know that they must also keep an eye on how coaching affects the organization, especially when the work is done in a context where the organization is expecting some outcome from the services.

Coaching sometimes can be a mix of ethnographic interviewing (a qualitative technique discussed in the next chapter), applying a business specialist approach, and a therapist role. This provides a unique opportunity for those with both a background in business and therapy—and although it is not necessary, it can be enhanced further if the coach also has a background in qualitative and/or quantitative research methods.

O'Neill (2000) identified the "typical" activities that coaches provide:

◊ Sharing conceptual frameworks, images, and metaphors

◊ Encouraging rigor in organizing, thinking, visioning, planning, and expectations

◊ Challenging executives to "competence or their learning edge"—terms akin to reaching excellence in their work

◊ Building a leader's capacity to manage his or her own anxiety in tough situations

Witherspoon and White's (1996) definition of consulting roles may be helpful here to broaden these roles of the coach to include consulting: first for skills, second for performance, third for development, or finally for the executive's agenda. Whatever the reason the coach was hired, it is critical at the outset to set the goals for the coaching process and the parameters of the coach's availability and role, and to revisit these periodically. These should be put into a memorandum of understanding, a contract, or proposal. This then forms the baseline for what kind of relationship and tasks will develop. Modes of coaching vary widely: some are phone consultations supported by email access, and others are face-to-face meetings at the consultant's office, the business, or a neutral site.

||||||||||||||||||

The number of resources for those who want to make coaching a central part of their work is expanding rapidly. For those who will work with senior executives or their teams, I would recommend giving attention to the following authors whose books are cited in the reference section: Sheth and Sobel, Lencioni, Covey, Morell and Chapperell, and finally Silberman. Many books and trainings are being offered. Certification programs have developed, notably from the College of Executive Coaching, the Center for Executive Coaching, and other training programs sanctioned by the International Coach Federation. Although there is no current requirement to have this credential, those in the field whom I have talked to believe it is a valuable goal to achieve and that it may be a necessity in the future. Consultants often effectively act as coaches to leaders and may use these skills as a part of a contract; so preparation, either from life experiences or training, may be of great help to your work as a consultant.

Additional resources are available at www. hsystemsconsutling.com/ training.php.
Links to these (and more) programs are at www.hsystemsconsulting. com/resources.php

A Special Case: Family-Based Businesses

Family-based businesses are by their very nature suited to the work of therapists in general and Marriage and Family Therapists in particular—especially those trained in systemic approaches. Social workers and counselors may thrive here but may, depending upon their training and experience, need to augment their knowledge of family systems or group dynamics. The complicated interplay of the business and the family provides for a unique intensity, and consultants need specific skills and training in the dynamics of families and organizations to be prepared.

Matheny and Zimmerman (2001) citing Friedman (1986) identified two areas that due to their emotional intensity are specialty areas for MFTs: family-based businesses and behavioral health agencies. To this list I would add ecclesiastical entities, which also share an emotional environment more intense than typical business environments. McClendon and Kadis (2004) note two cases where intervention by an MFT may be necessary: oppressive systems or disengaged systems.

Gordon and Nicholson (2008), in their book on conflict within family businesses, state this: "In family businesses some of the most powerful and helpful interventions come from advisers with a background in family therapy who are able to help families develop healthy communications and emotional self-discipline."

Family-based business does not mean "small business"; in fact, various estimates of the number of businesses worldwide that are family-based often are in the 90 percent or higher range. In the United States, Gersick and colleagues (1997) estimate the percentage at 65 to 80 percent.

More than 40 percent of the *Fortune 500*, as of 1997, were family-based businesses. However, most of these family-based businesses are owned by one person or couple and only 5 percent will survive into the third generation. How can a consultant who wants to work with family-based businesses understand their unique complexity? For that we turn to the work of the experts.

Gersick, critiquing earlier models, provided a useful comment when he noted that family-based businesses consist of three (as opposed to only two) overlapping parts or dimensions that need to be considered: the business (management) dimension, the family dimension, and the ownership dimension. This has been expanded by other theorists to include a significant number of other dimensions, but Gersick's model, I believe, is the most useful for both insight and clarity, so I present some of these ideas as a foundation for working with family-based businesses.

Gersick's model is essentially a developmental one. He is essentially asking, "How can we understand family-based businesses as they change over the course of time in each to these three dimensions?" The model then focuses on defining the stages of each dimension and the impact that these developmental tasks have on the family and the business as seen through the overlapping dimensions. Let's take a brief look at each of these in succession.

The business dimension. Understanding that businesses develop over time and that these changes create predictable traits and challenges in each stage is important for a family-based business consultant. While a full understanding of these issues would be a book by itself, in the following section I will give you a thumbnail of Gersick's model and discuss the traits of each dimension to develop an awareness of the need to understand family-based businesses in a sophisticated way. If you choose to operate in the area of family-based businesses, you will need to rely on other resources, some of which are listed in the references at the end of the book, to gain sufficient competence.

In Gersick's model the business dimension has three stages. First, start-up. Second, expansion/formalization. Third, maturity. A start-up business is necessarily concerned primarily with survival. Control typically is concentrated in the hands of one person or couple. Managing cash flow is critical. The products or services offered are limited. The customer base is quite small. The "big idea" of the company is often constrained by the realities of starting a new business. These traits all impact how the business will operate.

As the company grows, concerns about survival often decrease, product or service offerings become more complex, business practices and systems are formalized, and routines are established. At the same time employees may be added, and internal structures (divisions, work teams) may be created. The customer base may increase and the need to reach out to expanded or new markets may create a need for new processes, such as a marketing department, strategic planning, and higher-level financial management. Eventually, if the business survives, they reach maturity and have all the structure, processes, and trappings of a large business: a board of advisors, professional partners (accountants, lawyers), a loyal customer base, and the need to manage a complex financial picture. If the customer base is shrinking or there is a demand for continued growth, there may be pressure to expand the scope of the business or dramatic reformulations of the existing business.

The family dimension. Here Gersick has four stages: the young business family, entering the business, working together, and passing the baton. This may be the most comfortable dimension for therapists. We know the traits of young families, mid-life families, and aging families. However, we sometimes do not think about the impact of being in a family-based business and the developmental process that precipitates.

Young business families are often, depending upon the developmental stage of the business, putting a great deal of effort into developing a career or business, creating a strong marital relationship, and raising a family. In the "entering the business" phase, the parental dyad may be wrestling with issues related to their children's future, either in- or outside the family business, and with issues of separation and connection. At the "working together" stage, parents and children are often engaged in the business, with all its challenges to relationships, roles, and business practices. Learning how to work together, make decisions, and resolve conflict are paramount. And finally, there is a need for succession during the "passing the baton" stage.

The ownership dimension. In this dimension Gersick notes three developmental stages: controlling owner companies, sibling partnerships, and cousin consortiums. Family-based businesses typically start as controlling owner companies—that is, the ownership is concentrated in one individual or couple, as stated earlier. Capitalization of the business, balancing control and input from key stakeholders, and making decisions on the ownership structure for the next generation are all tasks to be accomplished in this stage. Sibling partnerships are defined by two or more siblings sharing ownership. Control has now spread from Mom and/or Dad to a pair (or more) of sisters and/or brothers.

The relationships among these siblings and the continued influence of their parents have a vital impact on how the business and family will operate. Challenges include how to share control, what is to be done with profits, what will be the role of non-family members, and how family members will be involved in the business. By the time companies become cousin consortiums, the complexity of the business has increased to the point that there are many shareholders and a mix of family and non-family managers. The chief challenges come from this complexity—managing family and shareholder groups and making decisions about family capital.

McClendon and Kadis (2004) provide an example of working with a family-based business in a four-day retreat format. Their case study and the activities that they planned would provide a comfortable format for many experienced therapists, providing a combination of working in large and small groups alternatively with various family groups, employees, and owner groups to make decisions about the future of the family-based business.

Succession. Succession planning, or the lack thereof, is often a catalyst for the inclusion of a consulting professional, especially one with a mental health background. Succession is a natural event for family-based businesses but one that is often ignored, mishandled, or addressed only in the event of a family crisis. The reasons that have been cited for this are numerous: the founders' fear of loss of control or death, the "busy-ness" of running an entrepreneurial venture, questions about the skills of the next generation, the branding of the business with the founder, and so forth.

What is clear is that a well-thought-out plan for succession benefits all involved: the parents, the children, and the business. Family-based history is replete with examples of failures in this area (Gordon & Nicholson, 2008). As a consultant you will encounter many more—bitter children or parents, battles for control, attitudes of entitlement and tight-fisted control. It doesn't get much uglier. A consultant who can help mediate a formal succession plan is worth the expenditure.

Tasks to be addressed per Gordon and Nicholson include these:

1. Transfer of ownership

2. Alteration of power, accountability, and responsibility

3. The psychological transition from one role to another

A therapist with an interest in learning about the unique world, challenges, and opportunities of family-based businesses would be well suited to working in these complex systems as a consultant. Awareness of the developmental needs and tasks, a sound understanding of family dynamics, and the business savvy to engage and support these systems may be especially suited to those with a therapeutic, especially family systems, framework. If the therapist/consultant can successfully navigate the transition from therapist to consultant—while retaining the knowledge and skills—the value to the family and the organization may be maximized.

Now let's look at a few other opportunities that I have run across in my work that are ideas ripe for a consulting niche.

Other Million-Dollar Ideas

The following is a list of other potential consulting areas (niches) that I have identified in my work—either through clients' expressing it as a gap in services or students' identifying it as a problem area they have experienced. Some or all of these, in my humble opinion, have the potential to develop into very lucrative opportunities for a consulting career—worth the price of the book in and of themselves. So, if you make it really big in one of these areas—remember earlier I told you that I'd hit you up for something more later—I'll take my Lexus in basic black, and thank you. Here's the list:

1. Contract with banks to provide crisis management after a robbery or attempted robbery. (You might be surprised to find out how often robbery is attempted as the industry tries to keep this quiet.)

2. Similar to number one, contract with retail businesses for crisis management and intervention

services. (Fast food and other businesses regularly deal with attempted robbery as well.)

3. Create policies and procedures for large churches with children's ministries (checking child abuse registries, supervision of workers, child safety, training and other activities. Many churches don't know they have this need until they have a problem and then they don't know what to do.)

4. Create a business specializing in writing grant proposals to support nonprofit agencies. (Successful grant writers are always welcome to non-profits and it is a skill easily learned if you can be detail oriented and organized.)

5. Become a succession planner for family-based businesses. (This is another area where there is a high need but if often not addressed until it becomes critical. May have to connect with financial planners or do education to develop as a niche.)

6. Provide strategic planning retreats for families running businesses. (Businesses regularly engage in strategic planning. Specializing in family-based businesses could set you apart from other consultants.)

7. Specialize in targeted surveys for small businesses (see surveys under chapter on qualitative consulting).

A Special Case: Psychologists (Organizational and Otherwise) and Consultation

In my experience, psychologists, compared to those trained in other mental health helping professions, generally have a more advanced awareness of consulting as a possible career choice. This awareness is a result of their training, which often emphasizes consulting roles—at least at the level of clinical supervision. This training gives them experience as a consultant in providing clinical supervision to students, which master's-prepared therapists may not get and, if they choose to specialize in organizational psychology, special training in the area of consulting with businesses (especially in the use of measurement tools). The PhD degree in psychology itself, along with other PhD training, includes education and experience with research methodology, which is certainly helpful to those who want to become consultants.

Even among psychologists, those who specialized in organizational psychology, with its educational focus on working with businesses, may have an obvious advantage as a new consultant over those who solely focused on clinical work. This advantage is primarily because the clinically trained psychologist may have had no coursework or experience that focused on business research, understanding the structure and function of businesses, or the tools of working with organizations. One might ask, "Wouldn't it be best then to always hire an organizational psychologist?" Not necessarily.

While organizational psychologists have an area of specialization in which they are best suited to operate, they also have certain limitations. First, in their choice to focus on organizational psychology, they may have limited clinical experience with individuals, couples, or families— the reverse of the educational limitation for clinically-focused professionals. This limitation, at times, can make I/O psychologists as limited as other kinds of consultants (accounting, IT, management) in their shortsightedness about the human side of businesses.

Second, for some the choice to focus on organizations was a conscious or unconscious choice not to engage in the intensity of working clinically with people. This may be due to some discomfort, lack of interpersonal skills, personality, or other factors that may make them a poorer choice for addressing issues that require a deeper understanding of human nature or interpersonal sophistication. No, not every psychologist is a "people person," as many of you already know.

It is said that Sigmund Freud, who received his training in the medical field, developed the technique of having clients lie down while he sat behind their heads due to his discomfort with interacting with people. If this story is true, it certainly seems to be born out in his relationships with his protégées, the two most prominent of whom broke away from their mentor and had somewhat stormy relations with Freud afterward. It seems that even those with great insight into the functioning of humans may not have the best interpersonal skills for dealing with those people—a critique that certainly can apply to some in the psychological consulting field.

To summarize, while this specialty area provides a boost to the individual in adopting a consulting role, and gives those trained in this way certain advantages and a unique skill set, those who have been trained in other traditions do not need to see their training, skills, or experience as a deficit. Rather, it should be seen as a unique offering, a different, but not inferior, approach and specialization to be applied to business concerns. Just as the organizational psychologists will ply their education, skill set, and experience to problems that fall within their unique scope of consulting so will those who come from other traditions, thus enhancing the diversity and richness of the consulting pool.

Expanding Your Tool Bag: Augmenting Your Knowledge and Skills

I have a friend who teaches technology courses at a local college. Imagine what it takes to remain "current" in this rapidly changing field. While his fellow professors in philosophy or history must remain knowledgeable about developments in their field the core of their field is relatively stable from one semester to the next. My friend's field is much different. His knowledge base becomes obsolete almost every semester. The hardware changes, the software changes, the formats change, the applications change—talk about being a life-long learner! While consulting is not this volatile, there certainly is the need to continue learning with each new customer and each new contract.

As a master's prepared therapist, now consultant, how can you demonstrate a rigor in your approach and methods to help you distinguish yourself as a consultant from the average therapist who works with organizations and to position yourself to compete with doctoral prepared consultants who have the research skills in their tool bag? Through continued learning and growing your experience. To start you on this path, I will next present a primer on qualitative methods, an approach that will assist you in adding rigor to your work as a consultant.

For those wanting additional training it can be found at www. hsystemsconsulting.com/ training.php.

CHAPTER 5

Qualitative Consulting

In the field of therapist-consultants, it is clear that doctoral-level professionals bring an advantage to the world of consulting: primarily a deep understanding of research methodology and skills. The master's-level professional—unless trained in this manner—may feel inadequate when terms like *qualitative* or *quantitative* consulting are used. But you have no need to feel inhibited in approaching a qualitative consulting process: the necessary knowledge and skills can be easily learned and applied. In fact, many of the skills of qualitative consulting are regularly used in your work as a therapist. What may be lacking for some is the cohesion of understanding the qualitative research framework and specifics about its methodology.

In this section you will begin to understand and learn how to apply qualitative methods to consulting. You will also find resources at the end of the book to help you further your education and apply what you have learned. Ready? Take a deep breath... and relax... breathing normally... finding your happy place... there are no statistics here, only the application of good interviewing skills and an understanding of the methods used to make sure the data collected are trustworthy. That's it in a nut shell. Only interviewing (have you done any of this in your career?) and techniques to gather accurate and useful information.

One caveat about qualitative consulting—especially for those who have been trained in a research setting—qualitative consulting with businesses and organizations often does not reach the lofty standards of academic research. This is the case for one very important reason: Most businesses do not want to pay for the cost of an academically rigorous process. If the business wants that level of rigor (and will pay for it), then by all means provide it if you are able to; however, typically this is not the case, and the consultant must make decisions about what level of rigor is necessary to meet the stated outcomes of the consulting contract.

Nevertheless, the skills and knowledge gained in understanding what is good, rigorous, qualitative methodology will stand you in good stead in making these decisions and avoiding pitfalls in your work. Thus the qualitative consultant must take on this task of deciding how much rigor is necessary to achieve the business outcomes without compromising the quality of the work. I will address this as we talk about the processes of qualitative consulting.

What Is Qualitative Consulting?

First a formal definition. Qualitative consulting is the application of qualitative research knowledge, its framework and methods, to the task of consulting with businesses or organizations. It is a way to gather data in a scientific way that protects the user of the research from interviewer bias.

Qualitative methods have been successfully used in many different venues. Experts on research tell us that they are particularly appropriate when four conditions exist, first, the work is focused on "discovery"—investigating an unknown area; second, understanding of the phenomenon or individuals must be "deep"; third, the context allows for multiple views or voices to be heard; fourth, the design must be allowed to emerge; and finally, the data desired are descriptive.

To apply qualitative methods to consulting work implies an understanding of the correct

◊ Framework

◊ Methods

◊ Processes

It is implied that one must also have a proper understanding of business operations, traits and processes to properly apply and interpret qualitative consulting techniques. We will begin that process (for those who don't already have this knowledge) when we address the nature of businesses and theories of human capital later in the book. For now let's stick with elements of good qualitative consulting methodology.

Applying Qualitative Consulting

Qualitative methodologies may be preferred in some environments (human service agencies. ecclesiastical settings, or family-based businesses, for example) over quantitative approaches, and at other times are used in combination with quantitative methods—surveys, for example.

Qualitative consulting, more so than quantitative approaches, may be a natural reach for a therapist who is already branded as a "people person" and not a "bean counter." Indeed, the fact that you have experience as a professional in a people-centered service can provide instant credibility in many cases—it is simply assumed that your understanding of people will translate to a better group or individual interview process with more insightful results. The assumption being that the therapist really understands people and what motivates them.

However, there is a downside as well. There may be a challenge in selling a qualitative service approach with some businesses. After all, businesses can ask questions, conduct focus groups, and develop action plans—so what added value do you bring to the table? This is precisely where an understanding of qualitative consulting can help. But it is also important to remember that there are several basic things the consultant can add that the business cannot easily achieve on its own, including the following:

◊ Broad experience outside this particular company

◊ Neutrality and credibility

◊ A unique conceptual model and process

◊ Knowledge and rigor to achieve desired outcomes

◊ Time and administration skills

The Qualitative Consulting Framework

The qualitative framework focuses on the contextual understanding of information. It examines processes and the meaning of data within the environment in which it exists. Quantitative approaches, in contrast, are marked by a focus on controlling variables that could confound the experiment of interest by having both treatment and control groups, using random assignment, and then applying an intervention (independent variable) and measuring its effect on a dependent variable. An experiment is conducted, an intervention or treatment applied, data collected and then analyzed. By contrast, in a qualitative (some call it a naturalistic) experiment, observations are made in the natural context and then the data are evaluated.

In this qualitative context, meaning as gathered in an environment is seen as multidimensional and dependent upon the informant's viewpoint. Data need to be understood in context if one wants to develop a deep understanding of the informant's view of the data, and avoid imposing an outsider's view. Data are descriptive and meaning is allowed to emerge from informants. Qualitative methods are based on fieldwork, such as one finds in anthropological studies of native peoples, and include the researcher as an involved, empathetic observer—rather than as an objective scientist working with laboratory experimentation and tight controls. A deep understanding of a phenomenon in context is the ultimate goal of a qualitative approach, rather than a generalizable finding as is sought in quantitative approaches.

In regard to consulting, the tools used need to be cast in the light of the particular theoretical framework adopted by the consultant. Qualitative consulting, then, is best used to seek emergent, deep understanding of a phenomenon in its fullest context. Findings are not focused on generalizing the results to a broad population (as in a quantitative approach), but on attempting to be highly descriptive—to understand the rich context of the phenomenon of interest—thus allowing application to other similar contexts.

Methods are likewise emergent. The consultant follows the data to deepen and broaden the understanding of the context, and the informant's experience within that context. Unlike quantitative approaches, there is no pre-designed experiment to be conducted here; instead, there is an investigation to be conducted.

Key Terms and Ideas of Qualitative Research

Providing rigorous methods in qualitative consulting is not easy. Businesses often balk at concepts such as allowing the design to "emerge" and the relatively time-consuming process of trying to develop a deep understanding of the issues they face. This is often where the consultant must educate the client on the value of investing in getting good data that will produce the outcomes they desire.

Researchers have developed methods for minimizing risks to the investigative process and improving the credibility of the conclusions reached. The good news for you as a consultant is that you don't have to meet the high standards of the research world to have something valuable to offer. The bad news is that if you don't offer a more rigorous process and results than businesses can provide on their own, your opportunities may be limited.

This is not to say that you must exceed their standards—often having an "outsider" is enough of a difference—but it can help if the consultant can bring a higher level of expertise to the table. Thus consultants using qualitative approaches would do well to pay at least some attention to standards of rigor as set forth in the research community.

In utilizing and evaluating qualitative methods in research, we look at improving the collection and evaluation of data through establishing or increasing the trustworthiness of the research by increasing its credibility, transferability, dependability, and confirmability (Lincoln & Guba, 1985). What are these? Simply techniques to make sure that the methods and data collected are useful and can be trusted. Referring to the work of Lincoln and Guba, let's take a moment to define each of these terms.

◊ Credibility. The match between the informant(s) and the researcher's reality. How do I know that what the researcher "heard" (say, in a focus group) was what the responder meant to communicate? Does the researcher's understanding reflect the full range of the individual's (or group's) experiences?

◊ Transferability. Placing interpretations in their proper setting to allow application to other similar settings. Where, when, and to whom does this apply?

◊ Dependability. Stability and consistency of the data collected. Can I trust that the methods of collection didn't skew or bias the data in some way?

◊ Confirmability. Examination of the data to assure that it is established in the informant's (not the researcher's) perceptions. A process of double checking to make sure that the data collected reflect the informant's views and opinions.

Now, practically speaking, how can a consultant use the knowledge of qualitative methodology to help in day-to-day work? By applying the hallmarks of good qualitative research to consulting tasks and analysis. To answer questions the business or organization raise, such as, "How can you be certain this is what our employees think?" In other words, even though the business or organization may have no interest in providing a rigorous process for the consultation (too costly), the consultant can use an understanding of good qualitative rigor to examine the likelihood that the results obtained will meet the stated goals of the organization and to interpret the results obtained.

How will you know that the data you gathered, say through interviews, were not biased by the interviewer. To whom does the information apply within or outside of the setting of the informant? Did the method of collection somehow taint the data collected? Have we checked the data with others to make sure that it accurately reflects the reality of the situation or context? All these are addressed by paying attention to the four concepts of good qualitative methodology just listed.

By applying these standards, the consultant can check his or her own thinking about what methods of data collection will best serve the client and help them reach their goals. How do you do that? Let's look at each standard separately. Please note that some of the methods used to establish rigor cut across categories and will be listed under each category but explained only once when it is first encountered.

Increasing Credibility

Credibility is concerned with creating a broad understanding of the phenomenon of interest. "How do we know that your information won't be biased?" or similar concerns can be addressed in this way. This means focusing on understanding the full experience of the individual, group, or phenomenon. Credibility is the attempt to integrate all "voices," even marginalized ones, into the collection of the data to reflect a deep understanding of the context. A number of methods to establish credibility have been identified in the literature; six are noted here.

1. Collegial Debriefings: One way to establish credibility is to have a consultant, other than yourself, review your analysis of an organization or business and suggest changes. This provides another opinion of your assessment, process, and conclusions.

2. Progressive Subjectivity: Creating a log of your own observations or keeping a journal of thoughts, observations, and data collected during the process help you to create a map of your own learning and how that affects later interpretations and findings.

3.   Negative Case Analysis: Stopping in the process of analyzing or assessing an organizational problem to ask yourself, "What data do not support my conclusions?" and examining what this might mean helps establish credibility.

4.   Triangulation: Using multiple methods to gather data helps to ensure that the information received is accurate. If multiple methods come to the same conclusions, then our confidence increases.

5.   Member Checks: Using informants to check your findings also helps to establish the credibility of the collected data and possible inferences derived from the data. This can be accomplished by creating a summary of interviews to be reviewed and confirmed by the participant, for example.

6.   6. Prolonged Engagement/Persistent Observation: Making sure to have enough time at the organization to establish trust, be able to observe and collect a broad range of data, and learn the organizational culture is important to establish credible results.

Creating Transferability

Transferability is the idea that the findings of the research or consultation can be applied to another setting, site, or group. It answers the customer's question, "Who does this information apply to?" Unlike quantitative approaches, which try to accomplish this through limiting variables that might make the data non-generalizable, qualitative approaches attempt to provide a rich description, and checks of that description, of the context to allow the findings to transfer to other settings. There are two unique approaches to transferability and six others (previously listed under Credibility) that also render aid to this process.

1. Contextual Description: Sufficient description of the context in which the data were collected, and from whence the recommendations come, to aid in decisions about when, where, and to whom the data can be used.

2. Purposive Sampling: Gathering data from a wide range of informants within the organization so that relevant aspects of the system are represented and understood. This continues until the consultant reaches saturation—redundant data are being received and no new data are emerging.

3. Collegial Debriefings—see *Credibility*

4. Progressive Subjectivity—see *Credibility*

5. Negative Case Analysis—see *Credibility*

6. Triangulation—see *Credibility*

7. Member Checks—see *Credibility*

8. Prolonged Engagement/Persistent Observation —see *Credibility*

Securing Dependability

Dependability is concerned with the stability and consistency of the data. How does the organization know that the information gathered yesterday still reflects the situation that exists today, or six months from now? There are four unique approaches, and two from the credibility section, that contribute.

1. Process Audit: Consultant carefully documents the process of their emerging work to enable a trusted colleague for evaluation of the project, how it was conducted, and comment on the process of the consultation (see Dependability Audit below).

2. Dependability Audit: Consultant provides their process audit documentation to a colleague familiar with qualitative consulting for a review of the consultancy process.

3. Multiple Methods: Using two or more methods to gather data from an organization in order to maximize the strengths and minimize the weaknesses of any one method.

4. Multiple Consultants: Like multiple methods, having more than one consultant working collaboratively can reduce bias and improve the quality of the data collected and interpretation of that data.

5. Triangulation—see *Credibility*

6. Member Checks—see *Credibility*

Achieving Confirmability

Confirmability is a check on the researcher or consultant's success at maintaining neutrality throughout the process. The customer may ask, "How do we know this is what our employees think and isn't just your own ideas?" It attempts to ensure that the experiences and perceptions are that of the informants and do not reflect the bias of the researcher or consultant. Here there are only two methods—one addressed earlier.

1. Stakeholder Review: Having all individuals who have a stake in the outcome of the consultant's project review and provide feedback of the collected data and findings.

2. Triangulation—see *Credibility*

Methods and Processes of Qualitative Consulting

What follows is a number of methods used in qualitative research and that are available for use by a qualitative consultant. A well-rounded consultant will have many or all of these tools available; their actual use is determined by the nature of the problem to be investigated and explained or resolved.

||||||||||||||||||||

There are a number of good resources (some listed at the end of the book) on the use of these tools that you will want to utilize if you are unfamiliar with these methods. Examples of instruments for data collection, including those for interviewing and focus groups, are provided in Appendix C. I provide the following as a thumbnail of the methods available and an introduction to their use.

||||||||||||||||||||

Again, Lincoln and Guba (1985) lead the way by providing an outline for the design of qualitative or naturalistic inquiry. Following is my revision and slight reordering of their steps to reflect the process of consulting.

1. Determine if the project fits a qualitative consulting framework. The consultant examines the goals of the organization and the suitability of applying a qualitative framework and determines if this approach has a realistic probability for achieving the goals.

2. Determine the focus of the consultation. This should be included in the proposal and include boundaries for the work, and provide criteria for the inclusion/exclusion of new information—additional interviews, focus groups, or other steps. These boundaries provide a range of what will be done in the project.

3. Determine where and from whom data will be collected. Will you interview senior executives? Conduct focus groups with business customers? Observe team behavior? A general plan is important, but it must also allow for the emergent process of a qualitative approach.

4. Determine what the successive phases of the data collection will be. For example, one might use open-ended questions, random interviews, or a survey initially followed by more defined focus groups. Here the strength of a qualitative approach is maximized, as the consultant follows the data to a deep understanding.

5. Determine when and what additional methods may be used, beyond the consultant as a trained observer. Remember that multiple methods, when practical, increase the rigor of the process and data collected.

6. Plan data collection and recording modes, including a plan for how detailed and specific questions will be, and how data will be recorded. Planning for the collection process and the analysis (including the final step listed below) at the beginning of the project is an important step and should not be considered lightly.

7. Plan the process and procedures of data analysis. This should be driven by the questions to be answered for the business or organization.

8. Plan the logistics of data collection. How will information be gathered? Who will gather it? When will it be gathered? What data will be collected?

9. Plan the techniques that will be used to provide rigor (trustworthiness). What elements of qualitative research are necessary to answer the questions for the organization or business?

Ethnographic Interviews

Ethnographic interviews grew out of anthropological studies that focused on understanding at a deep level the experiences of those in other (often third-world or small marginalized group) cultures. In consulting, this is often practiced when one or two consultants interview key individuals: the board chairperson, chief executive officer, senior managers, or others who are uniquely suited to provide good information or are significant to the organization. These interviews can result in consultants taking observations and notes on their findings, or may include a more formal process of interviewing, which can range from unstructured through semi-structured to structured.

Often early in the consulting process—let's call it the fact-finding or contracting phase— interviews will tend to be informal. You will simply use your skills of assessment and observation and, perhaps, record these observations in a proposal or management letter. However, once the project has the "green light," you must consider what form of interviewing will best accomplish the goals of the organization.

Interviewing key informants as part of the data gathering process is often an important part of consulting. Is it best to be unstructured (perhaps trust is a concern) or structured (we want to compare answers and attitudes on the same questions across the organization)? The consultant must decide and recommend how to proceed.

Interviewing processes and the method that follows, focus groups, are areas where behavioral health professionals can excel. Because of their training and experience in processing communication in many forms and on different levels, the consultants can often gather information that is much richer than that obtained by the average group leader or interviewer. This expertise, combined with knowledge of proper qualitative methodology, provides a very high level of skill in gaining a deep understanding of the informant's experiences.

Ethnographic interviews should be conducted with a plan as to the desired outcome of the interview. Is this to gather data, develop a psychological profile of the individual, understand a person's interpersonal posture, create buy-in for the consulting process, or something entirely different? These goals will help determine the best methods to use and the questions to ask each key informant. A sample interview guide is provided in the appendix C.

Focus Groups

A focus group is a method of qualitative data gathering that harnesses the dynamics of a group of individuals to gather data and insights into that data. This could be described as group interviewing, except that a well-run focus group will yield more data than simply the information that participants share with the facilitator.

In a focus group we may be particularly interested in sensitive information—that is, information that is not likely to otherwise be shared. This may be observed in the non-verbal behavior of the group, who takes "center stage" in the discussions, what disclosures might be discouraged, redirected, or minimized—there are many, many depths to the communication of groups of people that a trained consultant (here is where the therapy training is invaluable) can glean from a focus group.

Given that the consultant is aware of the existence of this secret knowledge, focus groups are also a valuable way to test theories gained from other data collection forms (say individual interviews or earlier focus groups). Are employees allowed to talk about this? Who looks comfortable or uncomfortable with this topic? Is there visible relief in the room as this topic is discussed? This behavior becomes part of the assessment, data gathering, and confirmation process in consulting.

How can you set up and conduct focus groups in a way that will be useful in your consulting? Here are a few guidelines. First, be clear what you are trying to do with the focus group. Is this to develop an understanding of the organization and a problem that has developed? Is the group tasked to develop an action plan to address a specific issue? Is the group part of the intervention—such as trying to gain buy-in for a management initiative? The goals will determine the size of the groups, the number of groups conducted, the data collected, and analysis of the data.

Second, after determining the goals to be pursued through the focus group process, you will want to determine the size and number of the focus groups. This determination will be partly practical: How many consultants will be involved? (This may limit the number of participants you include in the group.) What is the client willing to pay for? It is also strategic: How many groups do you need to conduct to fully understand the criteria of interest or to develop rigorous action plans, for example.

Generally, groups of six to twelve have been seen as manageable for a single consultant; this might be exceeded if the goals of the consulting warrant, or if additional consultants will be involved in the group process.

Once you have clearly established the goals for the group(s) and determined the size and number, the next step is to determine whom to include as informants. Here is where understanding the qualitative framework becomes important. In a qualitative approach, unlike most quantitative approaches, you will not be looking for a random sample to minimize the confounding factors (things that might distort the findings) and get an "average" understanding of the issues. Instead, you want to find the fullest range of experiences so that you can describe the breadth and depth of the issues for all parts of this human system. This means that selecting good informants is critical, very critical, very critical (it's important, you see). Start by selecting the criteria you need to consider in choosing informants. Then comes the problem of selection.

How do you select good informants? Here is a basic conundrum for the consultant. Can you sell the client on the importance of spending enough time assessing the organization so that you can select good participants? Do you trust the organization, with your guidance, to pick the participants—knowing your success is dependent upon this selection process? The path to take is often part of the proposal process, and your choice may be dependent upon your relationship with that particular client—do you trust their willingness to collaborate on this process or not?

A few things are critical. The number one consideration is that the criteria that defined the focus group must be met. This is true whether you select the participants or guide the organization in the selection process. A few basic "musts" should be considered. First, participants should not be either "yes men" for the organization or company, nor open anarchists plotting its demise. You want balanced, engaged, secure, trusted participants who will tell it like it is, good or bad.

Second, you want individuals who are willing to participate. Those who will speak up and share their insights, who care about the company and the issues addressed, and have some commitment to seeing the company improve. You do not want to choose individuals who simply sit back and observe but who do not participate and who care little about the outcome. However, it is also important not to just get those extroverts that talk easily—often some of the best insights come from those introverts who think before they speak, though they must be willing to speak.

Third, you want participants who will help you get the full range of experiences within the organization: this may include people who are trusted by others (in fact, this is critical), and who can inform the group of others' opinions or concerns, or the participants may be selected for their diversity (different shifts, job titles, opinions). The relative importance of each of these criteria will depend upon the goals for the focus group.

The next task is to determine what questions will be asked or tasks need to be completed as part of the focus group involvement. If focus groups are used to gather data, you will want to prepare an interview guide. This interview guide generally will include a broad, non-specific opening question (called a grand tour question), and increasingly more specific follow-up questions.

The grand tour question will be very broad and non-directive, something on the order of, "What is it like to work at this company?" or "How does communication take place in this work team?" In your first focus group, the follow-up questions will likely continue to be fairly broad. If the focus group is your fifth, questions may be more specific as you search for confirmation or varying views to flesh out your understanding of the full range of respondents' experiences.

Follow-up questions can be of various types, including descriptive, structural, or diversifying. Descriptive questions help you to understand what is being said by a participant: "Could you describe what that looks like?" or "Could you say more about how that happens?" They ask the participant to more fully describe the item of interest.

Structural questions focus on when, where, and who experiences a problem. "Does that happen on all shifts?" or "Where are the suggestions posted?" would be examples. The last category, diversifying, is seeking the range of experiences: "How does what you are saying relate to what was said earlier?" or "You have used two terms: X and Y. Are these the same or different?" The idea is to increasingly move from broad questions to more specific, targeted ones as your understanding of the organization and issue(s) grows. Remember the danger of interviewer bias, and don't move to specific questions too quickly!

Now that you're ready to conduct the focus group(s), what do you need to consider to make it a success? First, the setting and practical matters. You want participants to feel comfortable and not be distracted. The setting for the focus group becomes important for these reasons. Is the room warm and soundproof, and are interruptions minimized? There are potentially dozens of variables that could either positively or negatively impact the group. How long will the group meet? When will it be held? Will you serve snacks? Take a break in the middle? All these decisions need to be made, and their possible impact on your data considered.

Another issue that may affect these decisions is the impact of the business. Will the focus group be on company time or after work? Voluntary or paid? In our initial consulting proposal to the manufacturing company my colleague and I gathered the salary information of "line staff" and calculated the cost to the company of providing focus groups during work hours. I would not do this again unless asked by the organization to provide it. The company can evaluate this themselves (in fact they are in a better position to do this) and it is a negative from a sales point of view. (If voluntary, you may need to ask yourself the additional question, "Is this an indication of a lack of commitment on the part of the organizational leadership?") How far apart will successive focus groups be scheduled? Many questions will present themselves and choices will need to be made by the consultant.

Second, developing rapport. As an interviewer, it is important to develop enough of a relationship to help the participants be willing to share information, and perhaps even risk sharing insights or information that is potentially dangerous to them personally or professionally. At the outset of a focus group you must develop this trust. This occurs through your behavior "off stage"—how you greet them, interact during breaks and at the conclusion—as well as how you structure and run the group.

Part of this process is found in establishing the ground rules, especially confidentiality and how the data will be used, but it is greater than just this task. Are you a person who exudes trustworthiness, warmth, openness, safety? Informants will judge this as they choose to engage or not. Unfortunately, this is also predicated by how management has communicated and operated, both in the past and regarding the current consulting process, so you must be aware of the climate in which you are conducting the group(s) as well.

Third, the ground rules. It is important at the outset of the group to lay out the parameters of the group: the purpose, the process, protections, and how the data will be used. Participants will want to know the purpose of the group: "Why are we here?" Unless you have personally selected participants, assume that at least one of them will not know, saying, "My boss told me to come."

Review the reasons for the focus group and how it will address problems or opportunities within the organization. Tell the group the goals for the group, the format (length, breaks, recording data), clearly spell out potential risks and protections (share only what you want to be public, what is said here stays here, no names will be shared with management), and finally, inform them how their data will be used.

Fourth, recording data. Focus groups can produce a lot of data in a short time. How do you capture such richness? There are several options. One is to record the group(s).

You can rent or buy microphones designed to record groups (such as board meetings) using a conventional tape recorder or computer. This provides you with the luxury of reviewing the comments "live" after the group session has ended. You may also have the recordings transcribed for further review or analysis. This is an approach taken often in qualitative research. The downside? Transcribing takes time and costs money. Using these documents to increase the rigor of your analysis may provide the strongest method, but businesses may balk at paying for this type of rigor. Other approaches, less labor intensive and depending upon your goals, may be "good enough" or even advantageous. These other approaches may include having a second consultant who takes notes on comments, behavior, and interactions; using in vivo recording–such as using a flip pad to record comments and posting the "notes" around the walls of the room as you work—with the group (such as brainstorming or creating action plans); or scheduling time immediately after each group to record your own thoughts and impressions of the group's dynamics, behavior, and areas to further explore.

Fifth, follow up. Participants need to understand how their information will be used, as I said earlier, but they also need to know what will happen as a result of their work in the focus group. How will management communicate the results of the focus groups or any decisions made based on this data? When can they expect action to be taken? Often this is as much a part of the intervention of consulting as any other step. Helping to make actions visible, communicate, and be accountable are all important aspects that the organization may have failed in the past, or are presently failing, to provide for employees.

Sixth, analyzing the data. As with other aspects of qualitative consulting, the analysis of the data may be less rigorous in practice than it would be in an academic setting, although there is no reason that it couldn't be just as stringent. In the academic world, transcripts would be created and each subjected to a qualitative analysis. One such method would be to read through the transcripts several times, pick out key ideas, phrases, or words, then follow a process to cluster these ideas into categories (things employees like, things that frustrate employees). The researcher would then repeat this with other transcripts, finally combining all this data into larger domains (satisfaction with management practices).

In the fast-moving world of consulting, you must ask yourself, "How much analysis is needed to reach the goals of the organization?" Err on the side of too much, not too little rigor. If you use multiple methods and find that one would have been sufficient, then little harm is done. However, if you collect only the surface impressions and do not deeply understand the issues being focused on, then your work may fail to meet the goals of the contract.

If you recorded the focus groups, listen to the recordings several times. Make notes of common and uncommon themes, as well as the description, structure, and divergence of these themes. Develop follow-up questions for later groups, individual interviews, or as feedback to management (these represent areas to explore for the consultant that will be adopted, discarded, or modified as the work unfolds). Compare the notes you made with other data you have collected. Have a colleague read the transcripts and highlight the common and uncommon ideas they note. Compare these with your own analysis. If you didn't record, but took notes (flip chart) during or after the group, then review these several times and engage in a similar process. If a colleague was involved, do this separately and then compare your analyses.

The point of all this is to try and increase the likelihood that your results will have fidelity with the participants' views, develop some insight into those views, and be able to communicate them in an organized and useful manner.

Qualitative consulting methods can be a powerful approach for working with organizations and, if used with understanding and skill, can separate you as a consultant with a unique approach and skill set useful to a wide range of organizations and businesses. This method however contains a flexibility that must be accounted for in the development of proposals and contracts, a topic we will discuss next.

Surveys

A nice add-on to qualitative consulting is the use of a quantitative approach—the survey. Once again, as noted earlier, large consulting firms may hold a distinct advantage in applying any quantitative methods because of their ability to compare results on a large scale (national norms) or within the industry (other hospitals, for example). However, this need not completely rule out the use of quantitative approaches. The advantage they hold in having national data and large data sets also makes them likely to want to default to those surveys rather than craft a new, targeted survey— especially if it is for a "small" customer.

Here lies a gap that you could focus on as a population to serve; after all, well-run small businesses tend to grow. Even if you don't want to risk making this a primary product in your work, the survey may be just what is needed to gather appropriate data, to provide multiple instruments to gain that data, or to meet a client's needs. When is it appropriate? When you don't want to compare your data to a larger population (unless you use a standardized instrument with published norms, which is fine) but do want to look at the average employee, manager, or customer. They are also useful if you want to compare opinions across time, say employee satisfaction on an annual basis.

As a consultant you will want to refer to a good resource for the development, pilot testing, implementing, and analyzing of the results of the survey (Salant & Dillman, 1994) and, if your background is limited in research methods, you may need to retain the services of an expert in research (yes, a PhD) or statistician. If your project allows for, or would be enhanced by, an online instrument—or perhaps you wish to collect data from a larger or anonymous population—then you might want to utilize one of the many internet sources (Sue & Ritter, 2007). There are many to choose from and they are increasing their ability to help with designing, implementing, and analyzing the data from the survey. With some effort in this area, you can become proficient at designing these instruments, even if you choose to leave the number crunching to someone else.

A Manufacturing Example

Remember how I got started in consulting? I summarized the story earlier in the book. Let's go back to that and talk about how that consulting project unfolded and how the principles and practices of qualitative consulting—particularly a focus group approach supported by ethnographic interviews— were brought to bear in that case. On the way, I will discuss some of the issues in providing qualitative consulting as an educational endeavor, to help you see it in action and clarify the vision of providing qualitative consulting to businesses.

To recap: my colleague and I, both doctoral students, decided to do a research project in the area of qualitative consulting. My colleague had a longstanding Employee Assistance Program (EAP) contract with the organization, a large international agricultural manufacturing company, and had developed a relationship with the president of this family-owned business. My colleague approached the president with the tentative idea of doing a research project at the company to help improve employee satisfaction—a need that my colleague first identified, and that we both had seen in the EAP work at my colleague's clinic. This was accepted by the president and a meeting was arranged. The meeting was conducted with the president, myself, my colleague, our major professor, and the professor's wife (also a PhD consultant) to formalize an agreement and to begin to define the project.

The first meeting was with the president: a middle-aged man and son of the visionary father who had invented a machine that revolutionized one aspect of agricultural practice and had built the business into a multi-million-dollar international company. The current president and his sister, who ran the company, were known as approachable, conscientious, caring, and socially conscious by the employees generally, and were well-respected within the community (partly based on the creation of a family foundation, which supported many improvements in their home town). This first meeting was with the president alone.

We discussed the problem as we had identified it (employee satisfaction), discussed how we might apply qualitative methods (specifying what and where the problems existed and supplying ideas for resolution), and sold him on the ideas of deeply understanding the issues and letting the process emerge. The conclusion was that we would develop a proposal outlining our ideas, suggest a plan for proceeding, and estimate the associated costs of the project.

The proposal had several pieces: First, conduct a day-long tour of the facilities, guided by a chosen informant, and interview key individuals to gain a thorough understanding of the organization; second, identify informants to be included in focus groups; third, use the focus groups to identify key issues and remedies; and finally, report findings to upper management. The number of focus groups was to remain open due to the emergent nature of the inquiry. Informants were to be chosen by the consultants with the aid of human resources (HR), to make sure that rigorous data would be gathered. That's about it. No fancy processes or techniques. No high-level business language or cutting-edge jargon. Just a qualitative research process applied to the organization.

Our second meeting with the president included the HR director. He was relatively new on board—having started the previous year—but was definitely a "mover and shaker" who had already started some initiatives to address the morale issues, as we will see. His take on being brought into the discussion late was to try and reassure us (primarily the president, I think) that he was aware of the problem and was addressing it within his job duties. Still, despite the natural tendency to feel threatened by outsiders intruding into his domain (a resistance often seen at the beginning of a consulting process), he was open and supportive—an attitude which only grew, and to our delight proved to be his consistent stance—if not entirely up to speed on the idea or as of yet in full support.

At this point the proposal was accepted. Some comment was made, I don't remember by whom, about the survey that HR had undertaken with an outside international research organization, and a general question about dovetailing the work was made, but we proceeded with the agreement and scheduled the plant tour. We also discussed the best person to conduct the tour. In the tradition of qualitative processes, we wanted the best possible informant: someone loyal to the organization, but not a "yes man." Someone respected by employees and trusted by management. Someone who had a broad understanding of the company from different positions within the organization.

The man they gave us was Dick. Dick had worked for the company for almost thirty years. He had begun at the lowest levels of the organization and worked his way into a special liaison position working with the upper level of management. He was seen by employees as "one of us" and was trusted by management. It was a good choice.

On the appointed day we met with Dick. Dick was a slightly older man, in his fifties or early sixties perhaps, who appeared nervous. (Who wouldn't be? "We're sending a couple professors and two doctoral students for you to babysit for the day"—not my idea of a good time, and I am a professor and a PhD.) Dick expressed concern about what he was going to do with us "all day." Our tour, it should be noted, was scheduled from 8 a.m. to 5 p.m.

He seemed eager to please and anxious about giving us what we needed, and he proceeded to provide us with a good overview of the company, his history in it, and the current challenges the company faced in our interview with him, which lasted sixty to ninety minutes. We discussed with him the nature of our tour—that we wanted to understand what it was like to work in the company from a multitude of positions (the workers, middle management, support staff, upper management), and how these workgroups interacted, completed their work and communicated. He was up to the task.

The wisdom of choosing Dick became apparent at once. Everyone seemed to trust him. They spoke openly of their good and bad experiences with the company, and did so despite the fact that the interviews were conducted out in the open on the shop floor—where, theoretically at least, anyone could overhear what was said. From direct line staff to senior managers, we gathered our general impressions of the company, its employees, their processes, and challenges.

In an event that provided evidence of how this trust started at the top with the family owners (and perhaps reflecting their relationship with my colleague), we were even given a tour of the company's research and development area—the area where new products were being developed, and often jealously protected for fear of competitors taking advantage of their work.

The result of this tour and all the interviews we conducted was a summary of what we had learned. This summary then informed our next step—to conduct focus groups to develop a deeper understanding of the issues, when and where they occur, and to develop solutions for management.

In the meantime, things were percolating at the leadership level in the organization. The comment from the HR director about dovetailing the survey they had already completed with our work in using focus groups was discussed as a means to define and address the identified problems. Could our next meeting, they asked, be with these consultants, to review the results of the survey to inform our process? Our answer was yes. These consultants also planned to use their data in a focus group process to develop action plans for management—could we work with them and use our focus groups to achieve this outcome? Again, our answer was yes.

Here we were lucky. The consultants from the International Survey Research Corporation (ISR, now Towers Watson) were the consummate professionals. They met with us, gave us their data, educated us in their focus group process, and provided materials that they used on the back end of their consulting process—never once indicating any resistance or anger at these student interlopers. We even discussed the possibility of contracting for further back-end work for their company in the Midwest—something we eventually decided not to pursue.

The work ISR was doing for the company was focused on measuring the employee satisfaction of the company compared to national and industrial norms on sixteen broad topic areas from communication to leadership to employee benefits. The results that deviated negatively from the norms (the bottom five or six areas) were then explored in focus groups—the purpose of which was to discuss specific items from each domain (communication or leadership, for example) that reached significance statistically. The employees' responses that deviated from the norm were presented in the focus groups, and the employees were asked to explain the results based on their own knowledge and experiences. Solutions to the problems defined by the groups were then gathered and rank ordered by importance. The result was a completed action plan defining problems in each area and suggested solutions in order of importance to be presented to the senior management.

|||||||||||||||||||

As a side note—what was the impact on a doctoral student of his first brush with a professional consulting firm? First was the obvious advantage of a large organization in the application of quantitative data. *They* had national norms! They could compare this organization to data collected on other manufacturing firms. Second, as a doctoral grad student, I found, to my surprise, that the statistics they used were quite basic. No structural equation modeling, LISERL, or other fancy and complicated approaches (avant-garde approaches warming the heart of the modern PhD candidate). Nope, no newfangled cutting edge statistics here. T-tests. Simple t-tests. A statistical test that I learned in my master's course of testing. That was comforting. T-tests and significance levels—this was the most basic of statistics. I do not say this as criticism of the methods—it is quite typical in the field, as I have learned over time—just to comfort those of you who remember statistics as a personal Spanish Inquisition.

IIIIIIIIIIIIIIIIIII

Third, the focus group process did not have the rigor expected in the research world. This was a basic nuts-and-bolts process, to use groups to develop action plans—something most managers have done at times with their work team's input. My conclusion? Any small start-up consultant would be at a disadvantage in obtaining work from businesses who want comparisons with national data and quantitative approaches. But a start-up consultant could have a distinct advantage (particularly as a trained therapist and researcher) at applying qualitative approaches.

The next step was to get familiar with the data. It was presented in two forms. The categorical data were presented in bar charts comparing the company's results to the national norms relating to areas such as supervision, working conditions, pay and benefits, and others. The next level was the individual items or questions, which were examined for the six areas that were most problematic. Here each item that was significantly different from the national norm was chosen. These included items such as, "I know what is expected by my supervisor," ranked on a Likert scale from strongly disagree to strongly agree. The focus groups' purpose, then, would be to look at the overall results, discuss the specific questions contributing to underperforming in the six key areas, and identify and rank order suggested remedies. We'll come back to this in a moment.

We had already identified with the director of HR the characteristics that we wanted in our focus groups—good informants, much like Dick. The HR department, with agreement from management and the consultants, took on the job of identifying participants from all nine plants and each of three shifts. Again, as with the case of choosing Dick, they did their work well.

Incidentally, when my colleague and I did this again two years later, our groups were not as well chosen in that they did not yield such good informants. A problem, I believe, coming from our failure to formally sit down again, as we did in the first consultation, with HR personnel and go through how to choose good informants—instead we only reminded them—via a letter—of our previous discussion, the traits we needed, and provided them with a list of the traits. This was done due to changes in the demands on our time and distance restrictions at that time. One of the lessons learned when you work as a consultant, and a step that I would not now willingly omit.

What I hope this illustrates to you is that consulting is not some mystical process that only the initiated can engage in successfully. Many of the activities in consulting fall into a set of skills that most competent therapists possess as a natural part of their training and experience. Learning the tasks specific to consulting will come as you educate yourself and gain experience.

Qualitative methods or other approaches that rely on interviewing skills lend themselves very well to the training and experience of therapists. Any of the approaches listed earlier could easily become either a tool to use in a qualitative consulting approach or a specialty niche that you provide as a primary business product. Whatever your interests or experience, these methods can greatly increase your independence and income. Now let's turn to the basics of consulting—what do you actually do?

Here are resources for qualitative consulting: www.hsystemsconsulting. com/resources.php.

CHAPTER 6

Basic Tools of Consulting

The Practice of Consulting

A s you may guess from some of the examples and previous discussion, consultants do whatever is necessary and ethical to resolve a business problem. It can be that broad. More specifically, a consultant meets with business or organizational leaders; develops a general broad understanding of the problem(s) and a tentative approach; creates a consulting proposal; implements the interventions, services, and products; provides feedback on the results; and extends or terminates the contract.

Why Are Consultants Used by Businesses and Organizations?

There are a number of reasons that businesses hire consultants, but the short list includes improving the bottom line, performance, retention, effectiveness, and other interests pertinent to business and organizations. Often in my experience it is because the organization or business does not know what to do, does not want to directly confront a problem, or has failed to resolve some problem. Karen Grabow, an executive for the Land O'Lakes corporation, contributed a chapter to the *Handbook of Organizational Psychology* (Lowman, 2002) outlining eight recommendations for those who hire consultants. These recommendations were based on interviews she conducted with executives who have hired consultants. Her recommendations include these:

1. Consider carefully whether or not to call in a consultant.

2. Recommend the right group for the task.

3. Clearly articulate the purpose of the work.

4. Lay out a statement of the work and any deliverables up front and every time they change.

5. Assess credentials and experience of every consultant involved.

6. Have a single point of contact and frequent direct contact with the consultant.

7. Work alongside the consultant.

8. Get the information needed to implement the consultant's recommendations.

The bottom line is that organizations hire consultants to get the job done! Many of the concerns implied or expressed in this list—concerns that might prevent an executive from hiring the consultant—can be directly reduced if the consultant attends to the tasks of quality consulting. Articulating the purpose of the work, laying out a statement of the work, credentials, contacts, working alongside, implementation; items three through eight can all be addressed, and alleviated, by early contacts and a well-crafted proposal. This in turn will help the executive make decisions reflected in items one and two. In short, the consultant cannot control the decision to contract with an outside expert, but attending to the tasks of consulting well can reduce any barriers and improve the likelihood of success. Attention to the material in this text—especially the information on proposal development and contracting— will help you reach this goal.

Let's look closer at the concerns identified by Grabow's list. Restated, they could be identified as follows:

1. Should I call in a consultant or not?

2. If I decide to hire a consultant, who is the right choice?

3. Will we achieve the overall objective?

4. What will be done and what will I get for my money?

5. Is the consultant qualified to do the work?

6. Will the consultant be involved and communicate enough?

7. Will we be partners in the work?

8. Will we be better off after the consultant leaves?

Should I call in a consultant or not? A question every competent executive must answer. There is risk in "letting an outsider in." The outcomes are not ultimately predictable. Will it solve the problem, make it worse, or raise new ones? This is not a book for the executive; however, understanding that this is a legitimate concern for the executive and being respectful of that concern is important. Ethical consultants will be honest. They will recommend at times that the business not hire them—if the preliminary data gathering indicates that their services are not likely to provide the desired outcomes.

Grabow notes a paradox for executives: the tougher the decision, the more you need an *external* perspective and an *internal* buy-in. Hiring a consultant can give the executive the external perspective but may threaten the internal buy-in. If you have been contacted to discuss the identified problem(s), it is likely that someone has at least entertained the idea that an outside consultant would be a good idea—as a consultant, it is your job to decide if you agree.

|||||||||||||||||||

Once I was contacted by a denominational body to work with a local church that was having some significant conflict. The denomination had provided support to the congregation and had spent an entire year working on the problem—the problem was a difficult one and highly charged emotionally. Leaders were resigning and there were calls for the pastor's resignation (the focus of the conflict), accompanied by angry eruptions, church members leaving, and significant intra-church conflict.

At the time of the initial contact, the church leadership had developed an agreement on how to work together that addressed the pastor, the leadership, and the congregation. On the recommendation of a psychologist, who had been engaged to evaluate and advise the pastor, they had decided to contact a consultant to work with the congregation regarding the implementation of the ministry agreement.

The idea was that the consultant would meet with the congregation, help them to agree to the ministry "contract" and move forward as a congregation with the current pastor—who was not seen as the only or even primary problem in the church conflict, based on the psychologist's evaluation and the year-long interactions.

I was invited to a leadership meeting to assess the appropriateness of my possible involvement. In the meeting, it was obvious in the group's non-verbal behavior that there continued to be considerable division within leadership itself on the ministry agreement. In short, there were two camps: those who wanted to move forward and those that believed this was impossible with the current pastor. What does a consultant do? Should the leadership hire the consultant or not?

My position was that they should not—at least not for the original purpose of working with the congregation toward support for the ministry agreement. Imagine trying to get the congregation to commit to an agreement that leadership does not support. Instead, I made this concern overt: "If I am understanding correctly, there is still a division in this leadership group over the ministry agreement. I don't think working with the congregation in this circumstance will be successful. Instead, the leadership needs to address the division and decide if support can be developed to move forward with the congregation." This ultimately led to one leader disclosing that he had come prepared with a typed statement proposing the resignation or firing of the pastor—an action he did not take at the end of the meeting. Rather, they agreed to a six-month project to address the division in the leadership.

|||||||||||||||||||

It is the responsibility of the consultant, as well as the business's leadership, to determine if a project can be successful and to act in a way favorable to the long-term future of the organization and the individuals involved. This responsibility cannot be ignored or abrogated by the consultant.

If I decide to hire a consultant, who is the right choice? Again, the consultant is in a position to assist the organization or business in deciding which consultant, if any, is the right . choice for the business issue or problem to be addressed. Grabow emphasizes that the foundational discipline (accounting, psychology) should be considered in deciding whom to hire.

I agree. However, it can be complicated. Each consultant is unique. I've had a new student who "retired" from a career as an accountant—upon graduation she may be seen as a therapist, while she is more skilled and knowledgeable (at least initially) in the area of finance. Some helping professionals who want to become consultants may have never worked in management. Others have years of experience.

In short, while the business executive must decide who is the best fit, consultants must accurately assess their own experience, training, and abilities and only accept jobs that are within their scope of expertise. This does not mean that they cannot learn or stretch themselves— working with other specialists, getting additional training or experience—but they must believe that the objectives of the consulting project have a reasonable probability of being achieved. In discussing the business problems to be addressed, consultants must ask themselves, "Am I the right choice for this work?" If the answer is no, the work should be refused and the client referred.

Will we achieve the overall objective? What will be done and what will I get for my money? In short, will the consultant perform up to billing? Will we, as an organization, be better off after the consultant leaves? You will best address this question by carefully protecting your own personal and professional integrity and developing a high level of knowledge and skills as a consultant.

These qualities often are best reflected with new clients by a well-developed proposal. The better you do in codifying the goals or objectives of the consultation, outlining each party's tasks and responsibilities, and describing the interventions and deliverables to be provided—with the assumption that you carry all this out in good faith—the more likely the organization will feel it got its money's worth. The proposal is the roadmap and point of reference for measuring accomplishments. A solid, well-crafted proposal goes far to alleviate these concerns.

Is the consultant qualified to do the work? Will the consultant be involved enough? Will the consultant be a partner in the work? Questions regarding the consultant are judged in various ways. The first factor is the means through which the consultant was contacted.

A referral from a satisfied customer or trusted advisor goes a long way to establishing trust in the consultant's qualifications. However, you need to be ready to provide evidence of your qualifications. Sometimes this is a short biography or a list of other organizations or businesses you have served. At other times, this information helps leaders to assist others in their decision making. I had one CEO take the proposal with my biographical sketch and list of organizations served to his board, which he reported helped him to get a warm reception to hiring me.

Issues of involvement and a tendency toward collaboration are likely judged by the initial contact, exploratory meetings, and proposal process. How do you engage with the customer in the process of the initial discussions? Do you follow up on promises to contact them after the meeting? Is the proposal delivered on time, or even early? However, the proposal can once again assist in this process. Addressing communication and involvement, as well as reporting to management, can all formalize involvement and minimize the customer's concerns.

What Is a Typical Job?

Describing a typical job in consulting is akin to describing the typical business—a mind-numbing exercise at best. However, to give you a taste of what to expect, let's try to describe the process of a representational case.

Let's say you have been a practicing therapist in a community for a while. People trust you, and your clientele has slowly grown to include more influential leaders in the community. You have some limited EAP contracts with business entities or organizations. Then one of these leaders confronts a business problem. This problem happens to involve people and perhaps some element of mental health (otherwise the leader would call an accountant). You get a call asking your advice: "What would you do with a situation where... ?" You have just read this book and recognize this as an opportunity to provide some consulting services. What next?

First, don't be too quick to answer the question. Why? Remember that human relationships and interactional systems are complex. We discussed earlier how systems-focused professionals have taught us that the "quickest way out usually leads back in"—that is, a quick fix is unlikely to be a permanent solution.

Offer to make time to discuss the problem formally and at length. Listen intently, ask questions, determine how important the problem is to the leader and the organization as a whole. Educate the leader on the need for a solution over the idea of a Band-Aid approach and, if you reach agreement, offer to put together a proposal to address the issue(s). Ask permission to gather more information if needed and craft a well-thought-out proposal highlighting the need for a permanent solution.

After the proposal is delivered, you will either get the job, not get the job, or meet again to discuss the proposal—in the words of a popular 1970s song, "Two out of three ain't bad." If the leader wants to discuss the proposal, then this may indicate that there is some discomfort with moving ahead. Perhaps the proposal didn't quite meet expectations or the company's needs. Maybe it is a question of how to fund the consultation (often the case) and the leader needs more rationale or incentive, or wants to postpone until funds can be secured. Whatever the reasons, you need to understand (read "ask about") them and address them to move forward.

Once the proposal is accepted and the contract signed (often part of the proposal), then you are ready to begin. The path from this point forward is dependent upon the goals of the consultation, the work plan outlined in the proposal, and your own creativity. Enjoy it! It is an exhilarating ride.

Now we will turn to a brief education on the nature of business and its human capital (people) as a means to prepare you for the work ahead.

Learning about Business

Choosing to be a consultant to businesses and organizations will automatically jump-start your knowledge of business practices. Consultants are in charge of running their own business and must learn to manage business practices in many areas: financial, legal and taxes, management, marketing, communication, presentation, and others. The process of developing and formalizing your own business will provide you with valuable experiences for understanding businesses in general. In order to begin this journey, let's discuss a few important aspects of businesses.

Defining "Business"

What is a business? How do we define it or conceptualize its form and function?

A business (or organization) can be defined as

◊ A coordination of individuals

◊ Focused on a common goal(s)

◊ For the division of labor

◊ Organizing/ managing that labor

◊ For some specified outcome

Schein (1980) describes four general types of organizations. The first is those for the mutual benefit of its members, such as clubs and unions. The second is business concerns, examples of which include banks or retail stores. The third are service organizations, like hospitals and schools. And the fourth is commonweal organizations, such as governmental agencies and research facilities. Each of these broad business areas has special traits, and consultants may work across two or more types, or brand themselves to specialize in one type of organization.

Organizations or businesses can be described in at least three separate dimensions: hierarchical, functional, and interpersonal. Hierarchical describes the formal structure and formal power of the organization. It is often represented in an organizational chart. Informally it is described by the decision-making process within the organization.

The functional description is focused on how the organization actually operates. Formally, it is represented by program manuals, job descriptions, work flow charts, and other documents. Informally it is the description of what actually happens in the work environment.

The interpersonal dimension is, perhaps, the least formalized, yet often most powerful, of the organizational influences. Often described by terms such as *office politics* or *cliques,* the interactional relationships within organizations can have profound effects on operations. Yet this influence is often the most overlooked by businesses and organizations. It frequently has no formal structure, is ignored unless especially disruptive, and receives little or no thought in the formal planning and operations of the organization.

Yet, as we will explore in the section on human capital, organizations do have underlying theories about the people who make up the organization. These theories, and the behavior that results from them, have a dramatic impact on the organization, and often are the focus of consultants who work on the "human element."

Theories of Human Capital (Business lingo for "people")

Businesses have theories about everything they do. Theories on what makes their type of business successful. Theories on management styles. Theories on production, sales, expansion, competition, and so forth. It is no surprise, then, to find that they also have theories about both the people who work within them and those whom they define as their customers.

Managers and leaders also adopt theories and beliefs about what is called their *human capital*—a business term focusing on people as a resource to the business. These theories are influenced by their culture, the developmental history of businesses, the organization's philosophies and practices, and their own personality and experiences. Problems can arise where there are mismatches, failure to be flexible and change when needed, or when practices are particularly punitive.

||||||||||||||||||

In one of my consulting projects this mismatch became very apparent. The consultation was with a local bank that was having some significant issues within one of its departments. The bank president called and asked if I could intervene. I met with the managers of the work group, and I found them to be hard-working and loyal to the company. They were perplexed by the difficulties they were experiencing, as they had supervised teams successfully for many years. They expressed concern about the situation, the impact it was having on the individuals working on the team, and the team's performance.

Due to the complexity of the group, I included a colleague as a second consultant, and we met with the managers onsite and prepared them to identify some of the issues they saw as being potential sources for the problems.

After gathering the managers' views, my colleague and I suggested that the employees be involved in a focus group to inform the consultant about their views of the team, its performance, and management. The goal of the group was to identify problem areas, formulate problem statements, identify possible solutions, and rank order them by importance or effect, as feedback to the management team.

One of suggestions that came from the employees—a young group compared to the middle-aged managers—was related to increasing trust between management and the employees. Employees indicated that the managers, who were perceived as caring about them as individuals, often conducted closed-door meetings; however, these meetings over the course of time had become suspect, due to leaks in confidentiality or perceptions about the timing of when employees were called in.

As a remedy, one employee suggested that meetings occur in a different place and remarked that in his previous job managers would meet before or after work, or go eat lunch with employees to provide support for personal issues. When this was shared with management, the senior manager blurted out, "I'm *not* going to eat lunch with employees!" thus illustrating the basic mismatch: between employees and the manager. The employees saw the manager's role as providing (much appreciated) support—but they wanted a sense of safety at the same time. The manager's reaction, however, seemed to indicate that it was not management's role to be flexible in providing support for the employees.

IIIIIIIIIIIIIIIII

Those who have studied businesses throughout history found that there have been meta-theories in cultures themselves that often influence how businesses see their human capital. It is important for a consultant to realize the implicit assumptions that organizations or managers have about the people they manage. Employees and managers can be seen as trustworthy or untrustworthy, altruistic or selfish, self-motivated or dependent, simple or complex, and through many other lenses. To help illustrate this, and to prepare you for evaluating businesses' philosophy and theories about people, I will present some of the basic theories of business over the past couple of centuries.

The Rational-Economic View

With a philosophical underpinning of hedonism, the Rational-Economic (R-E) view of people leads to the conclusion that people work to maximize their own self-interests. Historically, from the beginning of the industrialization boom, employees were viewed as trying to increase their income or take-home pay and thus motivated primarily by economic interests—interests that were controlled by the business. This view can also be expressed when economic incentives do not exist—for example, in an organization of volunteers where people are seen as being motivated by their own hidden (selfish) agendas.

The R-E view led organizations to focus on how to motivate people through controlling economic incentives. Employees were seen as passive "factors," since the organization could manipulate the economic incentives that would in turn motivate or de-motivate the workers. People's feelings were seen as irrational and interfering with their ability to rationally consider their own self-interests; thus, managers needed to design work to minimize and control (perhaps even punish?) the emotional processes of their employees.

In this view, structure and management are the primary vehicles of positive outcomes for the organization or business. Employees are passive elements that need to be motivated, controlled, and directed to meet organizational needs—needs that run counter to the employees' self-interests. The organization's human capital, then, falls into two broad groups: the trustworthy (often management), who are seen as more altruistic, rational, or skilled; and the untrustworthy (often workers), who are self-serving, emotional, and money-motivated.

The R-E view led organizations to be over-reliant on organizational processes and management to achieve successful outcomes. There is no doubt that this model has been used successfully in the past—perhaps most successfully when other factors collude with it: the economic incentives are judged to be extraordinary, equivalent jobs are not available, the organization has high status, or the social climate is punitively set against job changes, for instance.

The Social-Factors View

Beginning with studies in the early twentieth century, the assumptions of the Rational-Economic view of people came into question. Researchers began to notice a new factor that appeared to trump the "economic self-interest" assumption: the power of social factors. This change—along with the philosophies to follow—has continued to reverberate today, although it varies in its effect and in the transformational influx of newer management philosophies (Deming and others, specifically). The primary contribution of this view is an understanding that other factors besides the economic can influence employees' motivation.

In the 1920s, Elton Mayo's work and subsequent publication of *The Human Problems of an Industrialized Civilisation* (1933) shook up prevailing thought regarding the motivation of employees and its impact on production. Mayo's studies of the Hawthorne Works of the Western

Electric Company led him to conclude that informal groups exercise strong controls over the work habits and attitudes of individual workers, and that the need for recognition, security, and a sense of belonging is more important to morale and productivity than the physical conditions in which one works.

Mayo was influenced by his work with a group of female telephone assemblers who increasingly improved their output despite both positive and negative changes in their work environment. Mayo had increased and decreased workday length, breaks, lighting, and other factors, but this group—which had been specially selected, placed under one supervisor in a separate room—increased their output even when the improvements were removed. Mayo found that the cause was high morale. This high morale was based on being selected, having a sense of control within a supportive environment, and social relationships. This highlighted the importance of informal social groups for improving production.

Specifically, Mayo's study pointed to a new set of assumptions about human capital. First, social needs are the primary motivator and shaper of the employee's sense of identity. Second, the industrial revolution and mechanization process has led to a loss of intrinsic value in the workplace; value is thus sought through the development of social relationships. Third, employees are more responsive to social forces of peer group than to incentives or controls of management. And finally, employees are responsive to the extent that supervisors meet their subordinates' needs for belonging, acceptance, and a sense of identity.

In this model, managers need to attend to more than just the tasks of the work environment. Managers, to protect or improve their employees' motivation level, must prioritize and demonstrate a concern for the psycho/social needs of their employees as well. Mayo's work led to managers' accepting social groups as a reality of organizations and to focus on incentivizing group performance rather than to focus only on the individuals or the task to be completed. Shifting their roles from those of planning, organizing, and controlling to being intermediaries between employees and upper management. Management then becomes about meeting the social needs of employees in order to increase motivation for work.

Similarly, starting in 1949, Eric Trist and Ken Bamforth conducted the Tavistock Coal Mining Studies, which explored the effects of technological changes (coal cutting equipment and conveyors replacing small work teams) on productivity. These changes had led to increases in workgroup size from teams of two to eight individuals to groups of forty to fifty. The researchers noted that differences began to exist in perceived prestige based upon work function, difficulties among workgroups, and low productivity. They concluded that the disruption of the social organization (the small artisan groups) led to poor organizational functioning.

Perhaps you have had similar experiences. My wife, Amy, as part of her college work-study, was employed on the "grounds crew" of the university. The supervisor tasked the employees to watering details for the summer—standing with a water hose on bushes and trees for hours on end. But when he noticed that employees were organizing their work so they could be in close proximity to another worker, in order to talk while watering, he instituted a fifty-foot rule: "No one is to be closer than fifty feet to another employee." As a result, morale fell and turnover increased dramatically— yes, including my wife.

More recently, theorists such as Drucker and others have questioned a purely social view and the utility of the model, in isolation from other approaches, may indeed be insufficient in the modern day—nevertheless, the social needs of employees continue to be a part of the consideration in a modern business framework.

The Hierarchy of Needs/Growth View

Theories focused on employee growth as a primary motivator evolved out of the work of Abraham Maslow. His 1943 article, "A Theory of Human Motivation," postulated a hierarchy of needs in which human needs were stratified with those deemed more basic being "lower-level" needs and higher functioning being on a "higher level." Maslow postulated that individuals must meet basic needs before they will be motivated by higher level needs. The five tiers of needs begin with physiological needs (breathing, food, sleep) and rise through needs for safety, love/belonging, and esteem to the pinnacle of self-actualization.

Motivation, then, is tied to this hierarchy of needs. Employees are seen as desiring growth, though they will focus on getting the most basic needs first. People are viewed as primarily self-motivated, and outside controls or incentives may only decrease their adjustment or potential growth. The managerial stance is thus that an employee's self-actualization or personal growth is not in conflict with organizational performance; rather, it goes hand in hand with it.

Thus, in contrast with the Social-Factors View, management is less concerned with the personal consideration of the individual (social, emotional, or psychological needs) and more concerned about making work meaningful—which will result in an increase in the individual's intrinsic motivation. Employees must be continually challenged and provided opportunities for growth. Authority is focused on the tasks, not on the individual person. Work tends to be seen as participatory.

Research has, in fact, identified "growth" as a primary concern for many employees, and thus provides some validation of this model. This has led to the development of newer forms of management such as the Learning Organization Model of Peter Senge (1990, 1994), which has an underlying assumption of growth despite being overtly a systems model—the view which we will explore next.

The Systems View

Systems theory came to prominence in the 1950s and 1960s. Based on the work of various theorists, individuals in the fields of psychology and psychiatry, followed later by business, became interested in applying this theory to their disciplines. In behavioral health, this led to the creation of the discipline of Marriage and Family Therapy. In business literature, it led to the application of systems principles to organizations, exemplified in the work of Peter Senge and his focus on the Learning Organization. His seminal work

The Fifth Discipline is the application of systems theory to the work of business.

A systems approach focuses on the system of interpersonal interactions. The focus is on the whole interrelated organism, rather than on one sub-system or part. An oft-quoted phrase is, "You can't cut an elephant in half." This implies that a system, here a biological one, is so interrelated that to dissect it is to terminate the system—or alter its very nature. Assumptions of a systems framework include the following:

1. The whole is more than the sum of its parts.

2. Causality is circular rather than linear.

3. There is more than one path to the same result (equifinality).

4. All parts are interrelated.

5. Focus should be on patterns, not events.

6. Systems conscribe individual roles and tend toward homeostasis.

7. There are multiple "explanations" of events as viewed from different parts of the system.

Managing or consulting from a systems perspective leads to the following stance:

◊ There are no single right answers. Systems interact. A variation in one part of the system leads to changes in the system as a whole (sometimes to restore equilibrium or homeostasis). There is no linear cause-and-effect rationale superior to another "view." There are multiple places to impact the system.

◊ The system cannot be divided. The system is self-sustaining. It is meaningless to focus on a part of the system without understanding how it relates and is dependent upon the larger system. Focus on a part leads to "first-order solutions" that in the long run fail to change the system as a whole.

◊ Cause and effect are not closely related in time and space. Short-term cause-and-effect thinking implies a failure to understand the organism of the system. Causes are often far removed in time and space from their ultimate impact on the system.

◊ The easiest way out will lead back in. First-order changes (simple fixes) are often a temporary deviation that the system will "correct" and return to its homeostatic state. Opening the window to cool a heated home will simply cause the furnace to kick on and add heat; the system is thus attempting to maintain the homeostatic temperature.

◊ Things will get worse before they get better. Systems resist change. Second order (meaningful) changes often must overcome the system's attempt to return to the status quo.

What does this mean for managers operating from a systems perspective? First, problems will not be viewed as "existing" within an individual or group. Problems must be seen in the context of the larger system, and understanding how systems manifest dysfunction is critical.

When problems arise, the manager will first look to what in the system could be causing the problem, rather than simply blaming an individual component of the system without considering the impact of the system as a whole. A poorly aligned wheel, created by the driver's frequent bumping of curbs, may lead to the failure of a tire without assuming a defect in the tire.

Second, events do not happen in isolation from their context. To go back to the previous example (and make it ludicrous), the tire cannot be assumed to fail out of some internal flaw without considering the impact of the entire system on its functioning. Again, the focus for a cause will consider the entire system.

Third, there are many paths to solutions, but they must include systemic changes to be permanent. Remember the furnace example? A permanent, second-order, change would be to turn off the system at the thermostat—not to open a window, which has to be considered part of that current heating/cooling system. In the same way, managers operating from a systems perspective will look for ways to change the system and see how it reacts, rather than focusing on the individual parts as quick fixes.

Fourth, a change in one part of the system will change the system itself, but not always in a predictable direction. Systems adjust. One part influences all other parts. Systemic change can lead to unexpected results and must be monitored.

Fifth, there is an interdependence between the system and the definition of roles within the system. The system creates, defines, limits, or expands roles. Roles cannot be seen as separate from the system that sustains them.

Other Influential Approaches

While the broad philosophical theories just described will be sufficient for the consultant to develop a framework for how organizations view their human capital, they often operate in the background and are not what most senior executives are reading about or focusing on today. It is important for the consultant to identify the philosophy of human capital by which an organization or executive operates—but many of these ideas are incorporated within the leading management or operation models in use. Understanding these assumptions can help you in identifying issues and helping businesses remedying problems.

To aid you in your development as a business consultant, three other influential models will be described very briefly here. Depending upon your interest areas, you may need to be intimately familiar with one or more of these models, or with none of them—thus the brevity—so resources are provided at the end of the book to allow you to fine-tune your developmental process.

Management by Objectives or MBO

In 1954 Peter Drucker published *The Practice of Management;* in that book he outlined the principles of Management by Objectives, or MBO. Management by Objectives is a systematic approach to increase organizational performance by aligning goals and objectives throughout the organization. The goal is to help everyone be on the same page regarding the desired outcomes of the organization, to provide a means for empowering employees to achieve objectives and goals in a timely manner, and to track performance and provide feedback. Many of today's organizations engage in a strategic planning and performance review process that directly stems from this philosophy.

In Search of Excellence

Tom Peters and Robert H. Waterman published *In Search of Excellence* in 1982, which became one of the best-selling and most influential texts on business ever written. Working at the vanguard of American businesses, who were quickly realizing that the quality of their products was beginning to lag in comparison to their foreign competitors, Peters and Waterman became the new gurus of quality. The ideas they promoted—active decision making, being close to the customer, entrepreneurship, productivity through people, value, and others—continue to permeate the thinking of businesses today.

Total Quality Management (TQM)/Six Sigma/ Kaizen/ISO 9000/Lean Manufacturing/Continuous Quality Improvement/Quality Assurance

Beginning in the 1980s, American manufacturers began taking note of the quality control advantages of their Japanese competitors. American practices included quality testing only as a final stage of the manufacturing process, while the Japanese model was to "get it right the first time" by finding the source of errors and avoiding or removing them. This model has led to the reorganization of many manufacturing processes. It promises to decrease costs (scrap, remanufacturing) and improve customer satisfaction but may also increase training costs.

With many variations, it remains a very important influence in manufacturing circles and service industries (as Continuous Quality Improvement or Quality Assurance processes), and has been applied in various other contexts—such as schools—as well.

||||||||||||||||||

In other areas of the business world, new models continue to gain influence as well. The consultant needs to understand these influences and educate himself to stay relevant. One of the recent influences that I would encourage you to read is Patrick Lencioni's *The Five Dysfunctions of a Team* and his other works.

||||||||||||||||||

A second area that a new consultant needs to understand is the basic language of business—accounting. While this may not be an area of particular interest, ignoring this part of your education will handicap you in presenting yourself as a savvy consultant, limit your contract prospects, and minimize your usefulness to executive leadership. It is to this aspect of businesses that we now turn.

Accounting: The Language of Business

Businesses exist to make a profit. Even nonprofit organizations must have cash to stay in operation. Thus the very life blood of businesses is financial. While it may not be what some of us prefer to focus on, it is inescapable if you are responsible for making the business a "going venture." The following section is designed to acquaint you with the basic documents of financial management. You may never have to look at these documents, let alone create any of them (your accountant may do this for you), but you do need to know these tools exist and how businesses use them. So let's take a brief look at these basic documents.

Balance Sheet

The balance sheet has often been described as a snapshot of the business's resources and who owns those resources at a given point in time. The balance sheet traditionally has been composed of two sides: assets on one side and liabilities/equity on the other, each of which, "balances," or has an identical bottom line to the other.

To illustrate how this balance sheet accounts both for the resources of the business (assets) and who owns them (liabilities and equity), consider the following simple example (note that accounting principles are simplified for illustrative value). Let's say you own a business, we'll call it The Super Good Pizza Company. As a company you start with one pizza (let's make it a "Kitchen Special," it's my favorite). And let's say that this pizza, bought from a supplier, cost $9—paid for by $3 loan from your parents, $3 of your own money (private citizen, not the business), and $3 your buddy gives you in advance for a third of the pizza. If at this point in time you have spent the $9 and are in possession of the pizza, how is this reflected on the company's balance sheet?—reflecting the business's current resources and who owns them. (I'll get this phrase "resources and who owns them" in your head eventually.) To record the current assets of the company, you could complete a balance sheet as follows:

Assets		Liabilities	
Inventory: 1 Pizza (worth $9)	$9	Mom & Dad Loan	$3
		Equity	
		Buddy's Part of Pizza	$3
		Your Part of Pizza	$3
Total	$9	Total	$9

Thus for those accustomed to reading balance sheets, it is easy to see what the business has as resources or value: one pizza worth $9. It is also easy to see who owns this value: it is equally divided among your parents (a debt or liability the business owes), your buddy, and you (the partners own a third of the asset or pizza) .

Note at this point the business is essentially broke. It owns nothing, really. Mom and Dad will want their money repaid (at least if they operate as typical creditors)—or they'll take the pizza in its place. Your buddy is hungry and will eat his third. As the owner, you will expect the business to grow, or you will take the value out of the company (eat the pizza at some point, if it's still good; if not, then the value is lost to the company and owner). To gain value, the business must create revenue in excess of its expenses—it must make a profit. If it does not, it will cease to exist. The balance sheet is a representation of the financial health of the company or organization. Analyzing the balance sheet is like looking at an individual's income and property and comparing this with his or her debt load.

Income Statement

The income statement is a description of how the business has moved from one point in time to another; for instance, from one balance sheet (1st Quarter) to the next (2nd Quarter). At a basic level, it chronicles the revenue and expenses of the business during the time frame it covers.

Managers often use income statements to monitor their programs or departments, and senior managers use them to supervise their subordinate managers. As a consultant or coach, if you are talking about financial issues with a manager or leader, it is possible they might share information from an income statement as they explain issues they are experiencing.

On the other hand, as a function of understanding a work team or business, you may also want to ask to see the income statements for a period of time. This might aid in your understanding of the operations of the team or organization and also help you assess the knowledge, practices, and management style of the leaders.

Let me give a simple example of how this might help. As a consultant you get called in to help a team that is under performing or having conflict. You ask to see the income statement for the department to help understand the operations of the team. As you identify the issues confronting the team, you also notice that there is money set aside in a line item for training and none of this money has been spent for this fiscal year. You may ask what this money is for (is there an environment that stifles personal growth by punishing continuing education absences?), or you may suggest that the manager spend this money on a specific activity (a ropes course, for example) to assist in fixing a problem or enhancing the team's functioning.

Finally, if you are pricing work based on some type of increase in output or revenue, then you might want to see these financial documents. This could help you establish a baseline for the current functioning of the team or organization and demonstrate any improvements (increased grant revenue, for example).

Cash Flow Statement

Cash flow documents are a way to track the movement of cash in and out of the business. A business cannot operate even one day without cash, so the tracking of cash is an important task of business life. This task is usually assigned to a senior management function such as the chief financial officer or executive director.

Managing the Accounts Receivable (ARs or money owed to the business) and the Accounts Payable (APs or money owed by the business) along with the use of credit is an important fiscal task that senior managers must attend to in order to succeed in the average business. As a consultant, if you are working with a senior manager on relevant issues, you might need to ask questions about how cash is tracked, about the business or department's current accounts receivable, or about other issues related to the tracking of cash flow.

The Auditor's Report/Auditor's Opinion

In most established businesses, the business's finances are subject to an annual, or sometimes semi-annual, audit. This assures investors, stockholders, and grantors that the business's financial reports have been subjected to an external review and that its fiscal practices are sound—or alerts them to any potential problems.

The outside auditor "samples" or "tests" the financial reporting of the business through a review of a portion of the business's financial transactions and subsequent recording and reporting of those transactions. The final result is the "audited year-end financials" (or commonly the Audited Reports) and a management letter from the auditor to upper management. This management letter gives summary judgment of the audit and gives the business either a "clean opinion"—a statement that the audit turned up no significant questions or problems—or a "qualified opinion," indicating some issues with the audit. These opinions are based on a comparison of the business's practices and performance with the standard accounting principles called the GAAP— or the generally accepted accounting principles.

Individuals interested in looking at the financial health of an organization will be particularly interested in the annual financials of the organization and the auditor's opinion. As a consultant, being aware of the existence of this document allows you to talk intelligently to senior managers.

While you do not need to have a rigorous understanding of these documents, enough familiarity to know what they are, when it might be important to ask about them, and to adequately make sense of them at a basic level is a tool you will want to have if you plan to work with leaders or senior managers.

Now that you have some idea what you need to know about businesses and organizations, let's talk about how you can actually make the transition to working as a human systems consultant.

How to Get Your First Contract

Okay, I Want to Be a Consultant. Now What?

You may not like this, but your first step toward becoming a consultant may be to practice patience. Now I know that this concept, patience, is not a best seller. I don't see book titles on the best seller lists like, How to be content until you succeed! or Practicing patience: Your sure way to success. I should be telling you to throw caution to the wind and you can make millions in your very first year. It may sell books (my book!), but for many people this is not the path to success but to disappointment and disillusionment.

I suspect that those who have the talent and drive to accomplish the amazing transition will have already made the leap and won't be reading this book. Sure it happens for some people, and I don't want to limit your potential—maybe you'll be one of them, but for most people, in my experience, the climb to success is a more modest one—and I want each of you to succeed.

Depending upon your goals—to supplement your income or to create a full-time consulting business—you may need to start by (1) looking for somewhere to consult pro-bono or, perhaps, for pay, or (2) developing a business plan and beginning to save cash for your start-up process.

||||||||||||||||||

This second option (a business plan and savings) was the plan I implemented. It took three years of saving cash from "moonlighting" work (I have six children and am by nature risk-averse), to save enough to leave my day job for a full-time private practice and consulting. In the meantime, I accepted management positions, including one as an executive director, to prepare myself for consulting with businesses—this continued my education with the fiscal and planning sides of running a business, and continued to grow my management experience.

||||||||||||||||||

If you don't choose to be patient and take the second option, there is one thing you must be wary of, and it is the same pattern that afflicts many therapists who want to move from full-time employment into a private practice. The pattern is this: You want to make a shift to consulting, so you begin to take on consulting gigs in addition to your full-time employment. This increases the amount of your workload and stress. Eventually, you are very busy and commensurately stressed. The money is good, but it's just not worth keeping up this level of activity.

At this point you may stop marketing or trying to get new consulting jobs. New jobs quit coming in, and you settle back into full-time employment. The way to avoid this is to either adopt option two or have a business (including a marketing plan) that you follow, which includes a point where you will leave your full-time employment (based on revenue or other factors) and devote your time fully to developing the new business.

Your Natural Network

Your natural network is often the best place to start looking for opportunities. Tell people you know that you are moving in a new direction. Talk about what you are learning and how it might be applied. Keep your ears open for possible consulting opportunities and offer to provide the services for free or at cost as you gather experience. This experience can build from things that are easy and natural— providing training, for instance—to more complex and difficult tasks. Any consulting as you get started is a plus: It builds your confidence and your experience, forces you to develop a product, and starts your operation as a legitimate business line.

Pro-Bono Start-Up

Often the easiest way to get started is by providing a service for free or "at cost." As a professional moving into a new area and trying to build some sense of expertise, it is often useful—and may even be advisable—to get your feet wet in a non-threatening environment. Working for free helps to create such an environment. Think about what you already know. What opportunities currently exist? Do you know of a work group, leader, or organization that is struggling? Are there any of these under specific stressors or with unique challenges? If so, then you may have someone to approach.

But what if you don't uncover any current opportunities? What can you do to develop an opportunity? My suggestion is to get involved. Organizations or businesses, no matter the type or size, tend to have or develop situations that could benefit from a consultant. By being involved—really involved—you will, I am confident, identify opportunities eventually.

For nonprofit or other organizations, this can be as a volunteer or participating in their activities. For a business this may mean using their products, researching the company or industry, or getting to know employees and participating in any public events the company sponsors. Being involved as we are discussing it here cannot be passive. Simply attending a meeting is often not sufficient to develop opportunities. You will not develop an intimate understanding of an organization, create the relationships to build trust, or have your expertise known. Active involvement does all this and allows you to assess the potential for consulting opportunities.

Admitting Ignorance, or... Life-Long Learning

I don't know what you think of the phrase "life-long learning," but every time I hear it, I think of admitting your ignorance. In one of my doctoral classes, we discussed new (postmodern) approaches to therapy and one of these theories, in the academic tradition of creating new ways of saying old ideas, talked about taking a position of "not-knowing." I had to laugh—quietly of course, as we academicians do not like to have our peculiarities laughed at—because going to graduate school to learn how to "not know" is an interesting idea. However, reversing my earlier cynical impulse, I find that in this current case it is descriptive.

We engage in life-long learning precisely because every situation is different and *requires* learning. To be effective to a broad range of organizations or businesses, we cannot afford to prejudge situations or apply cookie-cutter approaches, which is what was implied in the theory's use of the term as well—again, not a new idea. If this is anathema to you (that means, "it ain't good"), then you should limit your consulting to something relatively stable that you can repeat again and again, say teambuilding retreats, rather than concentrating on work that requires continued creativity or growth, IT, or electronic marketing, for example. You may also uncover opportunities for consulting as you continue your own education and growth process.

The Paying Job

Okay, perhaps this is the topic that led you to purchase this book. "Finally!" you say. The whole point, after all, of this process is to land that consulting project and get paid. It is an exciting, and a terrifying, time. Questions may be swirling in your head: "What will I do? Can I really help the client? How do I bill?" Or, perhaps, "Can I back out now?"

No, don't back out—unless you truly have gotten into something you cannot achieve. Undoubtedly, you have already done some thinking about pursuing this type of work: perhaps met with a relevant contact or two, thought about problems you might address, identified a client you would like to approach with a proposal and hopefully begun to talk about what the organization or business wants to accomplish.

If you have had discussions with the leadership and have a conceptual agreement, then you are ready to create a proposal to seal the consulting contract. If you have made it this far, congratulations! You are on your way. Now the real work begins, starting with creating the proposal.

CHAPTER 7

The Proposal Process

Proposals: Consultant for Hire

The proposal process is the bedrock of the consulting process. This is where marketing, contracting, assessment, interventions, and presentation all come together. The proposal process is the *means* to being a consultant, but it is not the *focus* of consulting.

As many authors note, if you write proposals but do not get hired, then you are a proposal writer and not a consultant. Proposals are the result of an agreement with a client to move into a contract. Agreement should already be sufficiently solid before you put your pen to paper. To date I have never, really never, submitted a proposal that has not turned into a contract. Some took three to four years to get funded and accepted, but I have never had even one refusal. Why? For several reasons, I think.

First, and foremost, I am not out there "beating the bushes" looking for consulting work. My consulting work comes largely through the network I have already established or by referral from that network. When the decision makers already know your work or you are recommended by people they trust, it makes the sales process much easier. Those consultants who must try to drum up business, through cold calls or traditional marketing to unqualified prospects, undoubtedly will have a certain percentage of rejections—this is to be expected and must be considered part of the cost of doing business. Nevertheless, other consultants confirm that the approach of conceptual agreement prior to developing a proposal—a process I practice and will teach you—generally leads to a very high acceptance rate.

Essentially, you and the business or organizational decision makers need to have agreed to the contract prior to writing the proposal. This means you will spend time (notice that this is unpaid time) with the businesses formulating an understanding of the problem(s), the organization, the leaders, and their perceived fixes. This is time well spent. It helps you to decide if you want to work with this organization and its leaders. It prevents writing proposals that will not be accepted. It provides you an opportunity to market who you are and what you do. And it helps you to be seen as a resource if you refer them to other forms of support.

The proposal itself is a persuasive document intended to close the sale. It is like the salesperson saying, "Is that all for you today?" or "How will you be paying? Cash or credit?" It is the final act in leading to the purchase and use of the item. As such, take it seriously.

What Makes a Good Proposal?

A proposal is a persuasive document. Don't ever forget this! So what makes a good proposal? The short answer is, "A good proposal is one that gets you hired." This proposal is about them—not you. It needs to speak to the audience it is intended to convince or persuade. Remember, they don't care about what you know or feel, or what you do, *unless* it is critical to the resolution of their business problem. That's the bottom line.

|||||||||||||||||||

This proposal process is like interviewing for a job – only tell them what will sell you as a potential partner. I once had an interviewee tell me that he couldn't find the office where we were interviewing and had mistakenly driven down the campus sidewalks to get to the interview. While this was not exactly alarming (we had a campus with broad sidewalks and no curbs), sharing it didn't put him in the most favorable light; I should not, perhaps, have been surprised when he later called, after not getting the position, and bawled me out for refusing to critique his performance in our interview (an act contrary to company policy) so he could do better in his future attempts. Perhaps his sharing the story was predictive after all. Maybe "poor boundaries" were an issue for him after all.

IIIIIIIIIIIIIIIIIII

Your proposal represents you. What will this document say about you? That you are attentive to detail? That you develop a deep understanding of the issues? Or the reverse? I remember a new therapist who brought me a brochure offering counseling services: the brochure was of poor quality, and worse, it was printed crookedly—some of the print even beyond the edge of the page! She may have been a wonderful therapist, but my first impression was of disbelief and horror that someone would present herself so poorly. This brochure became my example of what *not* to do for my master's-level students in my basic counseling course— certainly not what the brochure was created to do.

The old adage "time is money" is especially true in the business world. Proposals should be concise. Brevity, presuming it still contains all the necessary data, is a virtue. Proposals are created only after there is conceptual agreement and consensus. They cannot be substituted for building a relationship with the potential buyer, building trust, or establishing the general goals and approaches for the consultation—they are a result of all this early work.

Proposals, then, are summaries of what you and the client have already agreed on in person, focusing on demonstrating your skills to conceptualize and formalize that understanding and a contract to start your professional services. The proposal is the attempt to formally "close the deal" and start the (paid) work.

If you have many proposals rejected (over 20 percent), you need to do more work on the "front end" to build a conceptual agreement, consider if you are presenting a competent and authentic persona, and examine your proposal writing to see if all these elements are helping to promote the sale of your services.

How to Get the Job (and Not Just Be a Proposal Writer!)

To get consulting jobs, the most important tasks, in order, are these:

1. Be a person of authenticity and integrity.

2. Develop good relationships with business leaders.

3. Collaborate with leaders to identify problems that you can address.

4. Develop consensus about your services.

5. Write a great proposal.

6. Work hard to give high value for the pay.

7. Follow up. Follow up. Follow up... always.

8. Ask for referrals.

The Cover Letter (or Management Letter)

Proposals generally are composed of two parts: the cover letter (also called a management letter, although we will save that term for reporting results to management) and the proposal itself. Often cover letters are the last part of the proposal written; it is perhaps because of this that they sometimes feel as if they were merely an afterthought. At times, they have the feel of a template and are somewhat rote. I believe this is a mistake.

Why would a consultant—after spending so much time building relationships, developing trust, gaining conceptual agreement, and crafting a general outline of a consulting process—not want to emphasize this hard work in the cover letter? It is, after all, the first thing the client will read. In speaking, you always put your most important point first: people have very short attention spans. You want to do this with your proposal as well. In fact, if you have developed a high degree of trust with the client and have a strong conceptual agreement, they may only skim the proposal or not read it at all. (Remember the "time is money" concept?) Make the cover letter the most personal, professional, persuasive document that you can generate—and do it in one page, preferably, or no more than two pages.

The cover letter will reflect the relationship you have with the potential leader (or whoever is the buyer) and the organization. The letter can be very simple or complex. Samples, from actual proposals revised to protect confidentiality, are provided in Appendix A and you will see that some are quite simple and do not cover every area listed below. This is due to the scope of the proposal, the relationship that existed (in one case I was a former upper-management employee of the organization), and the conceptual agreement already achieved: "Let's do it. Just send me a letter of the costs" (I sent a formal proposal).

These six items should be covered in a good cover letter:

1. The process that led to completing the proposal

2. The objectives or results the organization wants to achieve

3. Reassurance that the consulting process can meet the objectives

4. A general time frame for the consulting process and completion

5. The next step(s) needed to begin the consulting

6. A final thanks and more assurances

Let's look at each of these. First, the process. Proposals often get passed around, busy managers' attentions are pulled to newer and more urgent problems, and time passes; all of these (and others) are reasons to begin the letter with a reminder of "how we got here." For the consultant, the opportunity here is to remind the client why consultation was deemed important and necessary—yes, necessary. Remember those counseling clients who call when there is a crisis, but if too much time passes they forget about what precipitated their crisis and don't follow through with counseling—only to re-experience the crisis later?

Often businesses and organizations are no less shortsighted. A reminder of the process that occurred informs those who were not involved why the proposal exists. It also has the potential of communicating to whom the proposal is important to and thus helping sell it: "Wow, the CEO *called him* to meet on this problem. I better pay attention to this." Descriptions of how you were contacted, what the identified problem was and how it evolved, who met to discuss the problem and solution, how it was decided to go forward with the proposal—all these may be parts of this description.

Second, the objectives or results expected. Conceptual agreement on what is to be accomplished is a critical factor. The letter should state these objectives clearly. Depending on the complexity of the project, these may be the actual objectives to be achieved and measured, or they may be broad goals that are further defined in the proposal itself. Putting these objectives as bullets or a separate paragraph can call attention to them and help assure the conceptual agreement is highlighted. Stating the goals clearly provides a baseline for the project and helps avoid later scope creep (the potential for clients to add tasks not in the original proposal: "Could you do one more focus group?" with the added risk of losing potential income).

Third, reassurance that the objectives can be met through the proposed activities is needed here and should be reinforced again at the end of the letter. As before, emphasizing that the conceptual agreement either led to or identified this approach can be effective. This is not the time to be wishy-washy. If you are unsure, then it's time for a reality check. Is the approach the right one? Will the proposed activities address the objectives set for the project? If you are still not sure, then you need to ask yourself if you are addressing the right problem.

For instance, have you agreed to increase morale? Can you really do it? Perhaps you've trapped yourself by setting unrealistic expectations. Maybe you can work with upper and middle management to develop a plan to increase morale. After all, you do not control all the variables that may influence the employees' morale. And remember, neither does the management. Hopefully you can influence the morale, but probably nothing more.

Fourth, a general time frame. Clearly state your expectations for the project. When will it start? Immediately, or will they have to wait to have your services? When will the interviews or other activities occur? How long will it take to complete? All these questions will be of interest to most clients. In your letter, give them a basic idea of start, duration, and finish. A timeline of the activities will be included in the proposal and is not the goal here; you want a thumbnail of the timeframe. It can be as simple as a statement: "Upon signing and returning this proposal, services will begin within two weeks and are expected to be completed within six months." The proposal will outline the specific steps and when they will occur as I will discuss later.

Fifth, the next steps are outlined. It is amazing how often people fail to be specific in their instructions—remember trying to follow the instructions of that technological gadget you purchased? "By inverting the parameters of the gadget and depressing the function button in the manner described (*where?*) your X1 Super Gadget will achieve superior performance, which will greatly enhance the user experience" (*what? where? okay, whatever*).

The client needs to know what to do after receiving the proposal. Tell them. "By signing and returning the proposal along with payment for the first half of the project, the client will engage [Your Consulting Service] to begin consulting services as outlined in the following proposal. The second copy [already signed by the consultant] may be kept by the organization for your records."

Sixth, always thank your readers and offer more assurance. Again, reassurance is important. Thank the client. Assure them that they made the right choice in calling you, and that the proposal is likely to help resolve the issues they are concerned about. Confidence is important and needs to be displayed here. Samples of cover letters are presented in Appendix A.

Components of a Proposal

Proposals, as we said before, should be succinct, and brevity is valuable. For this reason, you should include only what is necessary to get the contract and provide a grounding-point for the work to be done. Businesses generally don't care to hear about your pet philosophy or favorite approach to consulting; they just want their business problem fixed or the organization, team, or manager to thrive and grow.

Remember, the proposal itself is a persuasive document: that is, it needs to function to cement the verbal agreement made with the leader(s) and get the contract signed.

Although the cover letter summarizes how the proposal came about, the general goal, the time frame, results, and maybe other components of the formal proposal, it is only in the proposal body itself that the details are described. Examples of complete proposals are presented in Appendix B. The parts of a proposal have been described in many ways. For our purposes I will include the following sections:

1.   Purpose

Why is this proposal being offered? Start with a very simple statement of the purpose. This may be as simple a statement as, "The purpose of this proposal is _____."

2.   General goal or need

The general goal or need for consultation is stated next. Depending upon the goal of the consulting process, this may be short or lengthy. It is important to remember that a proposal may pass through more than one person's hands— therefore, write this section in a way that the entire process is described, but only briefly. Emphasize the concerns of the business rather than your process as a consultant.

3.   Specific goals and objectives

The third section is designed to give a clear statement of the goals and objectives of the consultation. These often are best listed in a bullet list or table. The basic goals and objectives should already have been agreed upon, at least in principle, during the meetings with the organization or leader. It is possible that this could be tweaked after the organization receives the proposal, but you will save yourself effort and perhaps land more contracts if you do a good job of listening and getting these outlined in your first attempt.

4. A timeline, flow diagram, or other visual overview
of the consultation process

A flow diagram or timeline is a nice visual representation of what will happen in the consulting process. It is the section that often is most clear for visual learners and helps both the consultant and the company think through the steps and stages of the consulting process.

5. Results or benefits expected

This is the section that describes what the consultant hopes to achieve. Perceptive readers may wonder if this section was addressed in the first three sections of the proposal. However, this section differs in that as a consultant you may see other possible results or benefits that you want to highlight. This is where you can demonstrate the depth of your understanding of the issues and the potential benefits to the organization. This is also where you may be able to "close the sale" if you have adequately demonstrated a logical process that supports the probability of achieving these results.

6. Evaluation plan and procedures

If there will be an evaluation process, then those processes and procedures are described here. This section can include data collection processes, instruments to be used, and statistical tests to be applied.

7. Reporting or deliverables

If there is anything that will be left behind after the end of the consulting process, it will be described in this section. Often this can be a presentation to management, a report, or some summary of the collected data. (Examples of management letters and reporting documents are included in Appendixes D and E.) This reporting may include a paper document, an electronic copy of the presentation, or the data files. Remember, this is something you are contracting to deliver as part of the contract—a failure to provide it may be a breach of your contract and could result in the forfeiture of your fee at best and a lawsuit for damages at worst.

8. Pricing and contracting

The final section addresses the cost of the project and the final contract language. Documents for expense tracking and billing are found in Appendix F. A business or organization may have a separate contracting process, but if not, the proposal serves as a contract as well. This section addresses the fees to be charged, the payment requirements, contract language, and a signature block.

The proposal sets the course for the entire consulting process. It is a baseline to return to if any questions arise. But what do you do if the client wants to add to the proposal? You must be ready to handle these requests and avoid "scope creep," which is addressed next.

Additional samples of proposals, cover letters, and other consulting documents can be found at www. hsystemsconsulting.com/ resources.php.

Avoiding Scope Creep

Scope creep. We encountered this term earlier. If you are still unclear about what scope creep is, then you probably have not been employed as a consultant. Scope creep is when the CEO says, "Could you also meet with _____?" or "Could you help us with _____?"

Often additional requests come after the original proposal and contracting is complete—although it also happens frequently at the time the proposal is first submitted—and is something extra that you did not plan for in the proposal or (and this is of vital importance) include in the cost of your services. Even if it is included (as evidenced by the consultant's thought, "Oh well, I'm paid hourly anyway."), it can change the focus of the consulting, making you chase rabbit trails or muddy the water—all leading to potential failure to address and successfully meet the goals or outcomes of the original consulting proposal.

The best protection from scope creep is a well-written proposal and a carefully cultivated habit of consulting the proposal (and revising it) when any changes are proposed. Scope creep will kill your profitability if you do not jealously protect yourself from this stealthy intruder.

CHAPTER 8

Assessment and Intervention, or What Should I Do?

An Introduction to Assessment

For the qualitative consultant, assessment typically takes place through some combination of interviewing (meetings with managers, ethnographic interviews, focus groups) and observation. See the chapter on Qualitative Consulting. However, at times the consultant will want a more quantitative or formal assessment or intervention. This may be to meet the "multiple methods" criteria for rigor or be determined by the consultant or business leader's interests and goals.

Starting with the initial contact, the consultant needs to assess his or her ability to meet the organization's needs and achieve the outcomes desired. This assessment can be complemented by other tools such as surveys, standardized instruments (many therapists, for instance, have conducted team building with the Myers-Briggs Type Indicator—MBTI), and if you have access to or been trained in their use, other quantitative methods. Other resources (Senge, Silberman, or Lencioini) provide tools that can be incorporated in your work.

The consultant must always be aware of three levels of analysis: the external context that the organization is operating in, the organization's own culture and internal context, and the immediate context of the individual or group within the organization.

Don't be afraid of what you don't already know. As a therapist you are familiar with working with individuals, couples, or groups within a larger context (legal, school, intergenerational, or family systems). The heart of consulting, like therapy, is finding solutions to problems you have not yet faced. You do not have to go it on your own. There are resources (published consulting tools, resources for interviewing or conducting focus groups, and publishers of instruments) that you will learn to use. Another advantage to this process, as you will see, is that you increase your own knowledge and worth as a consultant incrementally by stretching yourself and your skills.

In contrast to the assessment process in which you may want to exercise a limited range of approaches, interventions are driven by the needs of the organization or business and can vary to a great degree. Intervention is driven by the findings of the assessment process. If the primary role of the consulting was to identify problems and recommend solutions, then the intervention itself may come from the management of the company.

||||||||||||||||||

In the example of the manufacturing consulting case described in chapter 5, many of the final interventions for the company, as identified by employees (such as increasing ventilation in the welding areas), were out of the consultants' control. The intervention from the consultants' view in this case was to conduct focus groups, create action plans, and communicate this to the senior management. Senior management then had the responsibility for following up on the recommendations for the company.

||||||||||||||||||

In other cases, the consultant may be designing the intervention for the organization. This may be through training, a team-building process, a retreat to address some uncovered issues, making management recommendations, or the development of new resources for the company. This is where your continued learning and development as a consultant is critical. Commit yourself to continuing to add skills and the knowledge of resources to your tool box.

In another situation, I was looking for an instrument to use in my work with a church's leadership group. The pulpit minister was my primary contact and had expressed a desire to use an instrument as part of a leadership retreat, suggesting the MBTI. However, I thought this team needed something more than just the administering of a personality instrument and an explanation of personality types. I contacted the publisher of the MBTI, explained what I was looking for, and asked about some of the MBTI tools for teams and leaders. The publisher's salesperson asked a few good questions and led me away from the team/leader MBTI tools to a different instrument (the FIRO-B), which combines the MBTI and an evaluation of leadership style. I ordered the training for the instrument and decided to go with their recommendation. It worked out very well. The client was pleased, I was pleased, and I added a new tool to my toolbox.

There are a number of instruments that therapist/ consultants have used in consulting work and many more that could, and should, be used. These basic tools can be used as a supplement or a primary focus in the consulting work. A short list of instruments follows:

◊ Myers-Briggs Type Indicater

◊ FIRO-B

◊ Leadership Spectrum Profile

◊ Thomas-Kilmann Conflict Mode Instrument (TKI)

◊ EQ-i

◊ Strength Deployment Inventory (SDI)

◊ Klein Group Instrument (KGI)

Although it is beyond the scope of this book to introduce you to the fine art of assessment, it is important that you be willing to explore these and other instruments as your consulting work requires. An unwillingness to learn and grow in this area can lead to becoming a "one-trick pony," which may limit the population of job opportunities for you as a consultant. This doesn't mean you should never take on any work that is new or novel—as you will see later—but you do need to know your own abilities and limitations.

If you face issues that you are not sure you have the skills or experience to address, you must be ready to call in other experts. This may include someone with experience administering, scoring, or interpreting a specific assessment tool. There is nothing wrong with this. You may need to advise clients to hire another consultant to complete a task you cannot perform. Perhaps this is to complete a specific assessment: conduct and analyze a survey, do strategic planning; or this may be recommending hiring a professional in a specialty area (such as human resources or organizing parts distribution). Admitting that this area is not your expertise, and making a recommendation, is still helping the client—if you already know of a resource you trust and can recommend, even better.

Identifying Your Skills and Knowledge —What Do I Already Know?

One of the first things I recommend to an aspiring consultant is to get a cup of coffee, maybe two. Yes, coffee can be important to consultants, but that's not the point. The point is this: You need to review your work and educational experiences to mine your own unique skills and knowledge. What do you know? What experiences have you had? How does this position you to be of value to businesses and organizations?

This process is not as easy as it looks. You may need a pot of coffee. Have you mostly been an employee? What was that experience like? What managers did you like? Which ones did you wish you could transport to Alpha Centauri? Do you have management experience? Have you run lots of groups? Done interviews? Worked as a trainer? Are you a good athlete? A speaker? The list is endless. These are your unique advantages and the key to your niche as a consultant.

Are you young? Does the list look weak? Cheer up. This can lead to a plan to position yourself to become a consultant—your palette is clean and ready to be mixed to your own personal liking. Remember that I worked into senior management positions after completing my PhD in preparation—which turned out to be a seven-year commitment—for launching my consulting career. It is worth the wait.

Rigorous intervention is beyond the scope of this book but additional resources can be found at www.hsystemsconsulting. com/resources.php.

Expanding Your Skills and Knowledge—What Can I Learn?

After you identify what you already know and can do (skills and knowledge), then make a decision about what you would like to learn. Begin to read on the topic, attend a training, or find a way to participate in a process with someone who already provides the service. Now is not the time to doubt yourself. Just like Thomas Edison—who said that he had not failed, only found 10,000 ways that won't work—we need to take the attitude that "not knowing" is a step toward knowing or succeeding.

Consultants need to invest in their future, building their knowledge, their skills, and their value as a resource; don't neglect this. Next we will turn to another important area the consultant needs to consider—what to charge.

CHAPTER 9

Pricing Your Services

What Your Services Really Cost

A s I write, I am considering having a utility trailer repainted. The shop that built the trailer, and painted it originally, has always been located on a family farm and is relatively cheap—currently $65 plus paint for the work. However, the owner is currently building a big building near town, which means that his price for the paint job is likely to go up when he moves into his new shop. Why? Because the costs (overhead) to his business have increased.

This is not some form of profiteering or attempt to cheat the customer. He simply will not be able to charge the same price and stay in business, unless he cuts his profit margin— which he should not do unless it is absolutely necessary. Yes, customers help pay for the type of building, location, paint—

all business costs of those they use for services and products. Conclusion: in this case, get the trailer painted now or expect a higher price.

When the plumber pays more for gas, you pay more for plumbing. Airlines will charge luggage fees and fuel surcharges. Businesses must account for these rising costs. Consultants, too, must account for the actual costs of doing business. New consultants, or therapists, unless they are coming out of the business or accounting worlds, rarely account adequately for these costs.

Most new therapists—and I think this also applies to new consultants coming out of this framework—ask only one question: "What do I need to make?" This leads them to think only about one of the costs of doing business: their salary. Expenses are an afterthought. Overhead—those ongoing costs of operating the business? No consideration at all. This is especially true if the costs don't exist at present ("I don't have a fax machine," does not mean the business will not need one in the future. The business should include this in its profit margin to save for that future need.) After all, most who are starting out in consulting have no separate office for this business. They use their home computer and printer. But they fail to plan for the future where they *will* need these for their business (maybe on the very next job) and must have the funds to purchase and then maintain these business tools. What about the time for marketing? Proposal writing? This time costs the company in lost production and must be included in the cost of its services. It is worth the time to accurately develop your own fee structure based on something tangible—a process you are about to embark upon if you will.

Leaving the "Helping Professional" Mindset

Once again, my experience leads me to believe that there is a preconceived limitation in the thinking of the average behavioral health provider. This is nowhere more apparent than in the area of fee setting. My plumber apparently has no problem charging me a relatively high hourly rate. Neither does my doctor or dentist or accountant. Building contractor estimates make me question whether to put off my home improvement project another year, yet many behavioral health providers appear to struggle and even apologize for charging reasonable or below-market value fees. Why?

Many point to the history of social work as a "female profession," and a culture that has undervalued females. Others talk of the ministry mindset, or views toward liberalism and socialism. Still others talk of codependent traits and victimhood. Whatever the reason, there are ways to be confident that the fees you charge are reasonable and not susceptible to momentary emotions: by determining your fee structure and sticking to it as reasonably created and necessary to stay in business.

As one of my colleagues says, "You can do good *and* do well." If this tension between empathy for clients and your need to make a living wage causes you emotional angst, then you may need a personal coach to aid in your development and keep you on track. As a way to start this development, let's talk about developing a fee structure.

Developing Your Fee Structure —How Much Should I Charge?

Perhaps no other early task of starting a business gets more emotional focus than setting the initial fees for the business. This can raise some of the baggage talked about earlier: "What if they are upset by my fee?" "Am I really worth it?" "It seems like so much, will anyone hire me?" But setting fees is a fundamental necessity of business. Good news for the worriers out there—there is a logical process to setting fees that will rid you of the uncertainty and lessen the anxiety of talking to the clients about it!

One caveat before we continue. You should also note that there is another line of thought in the consulting world— represented prominently by Alan Weiss (2002)—that recoils from the idea of a "fee structure." If you are more comfortable with a "wheeling and dealing" approach or have been in the business a long time and are comfortable with asking for (even demanding) payment and negotiation, you may want to skip the fee structure section and go on. If the idea makes your knees go weak or you are new to setting fees, then, please, continue.

In general, businesses must account for three factors in setting prices: the cost of labor, the cost of being in business (overhead), and a profit margin (fee for the risk of being in business). Subsumed in these are many things you may be wondering about: your salary (labor), advertising or marketing costs (overhead), and security for the future (profit). The amount of profit you can demand—and thus the reward of taking the risk of operating your own business—is predicated on several external factors, including these:

◊ The need for the services

◊ The skills/abilities of the consultant(s)

◊ Reputation and/or availability

◊ Sophistication of the product provided

Fees, then, are *not* derived from thin air. They are real numbers based on qualities of the marketplace, the consultant's traits, and business expenses. It is important at the beginning to realize that these are real expenses and act accordingly. While any particular consulting job may be negotiated—more or less time, activities, etc.—*your rate should not be negotiable!* You will build confidence by establishing a real and solid number that you can be sure is fair and defensible.

As I mentioned, to establish a rate you must account for labor, overhead, and a profit margin. Start by establishing an initial budget. Write down all the possible expenses of operating your business. Make sure that you account for all the costs of running the business, *even if you are not currently experiencing the item as an expense.* For example, if you plan to maintain printed brochures about your services as a marketing tool, include them in your budget even though you don't plan to print them until you get a few clients.

As a start-up business, you will under-fund yourself if you do not capture all the costs of running the business (overhead) from the start. This will make it harder to be successful—most businesses fail in start-up because they are underfunded.

The budget should cover several areas of business expenses. This includes costs that may not at first be apparent, such as the cost of time away from consulting to market your services. A sample budget follows to help you create your own preliminary budget and fee structure.

Consulting Business Monthly Budget	
Category	**Amount**
Rent	$600
Telephone	200
Copying	100
Postage	60
Mileage/Travel	230
Insurance	250
Benefits	500
Professional Development	100
Office Supplies	160
Equipment	120
Accounting/Professional	150
Marketing (4 days)	920
Other	110
Total	**$3,500**

The initial budget process is often part of a general business plan for the first one to three years, or more, of your business.

This begins the process of planning your business strategy, including the fees that you will charge. There are many resources for developing these business plans and budgets, and some are specific to consultants (Holtz, 1993; Biech, 2001; Horan, 2006)

Once the expense portion of the budget is complete, you are ready to establish your fees. As part of the budget, you have estimated the overhead the business will carry. Now you must establish the worth of your time, and with this you can add the cost of overhead and a profit margin to establish a specific daily and hourly rate for your consulting services. Confused? Hang on. An example is coming that, I hope, will make this clear.

First, however, let's define a few terms. Many experts have developed methods to calculate and set fees. We will follow a process and terminology laid out by Shenson and Nicholas (1997) and similar to approaches by other independent consultants (Holtz, 1993; Keoughan & Joanning, 1997). I highly recommend these resources for new consultants.

◊ Daily Labor Rate (DLR): Fee for the services of the professional consultant(s).

◊ Daily Rate (DR): Total rate charged per day.

◊ Daily Overhead Rate (DOR): Cost of business expenses as part of daily rate (DR).

◊ Daily Profit Rate (DPR): Cost of risk as part of daily rate (DR).

◊ Hourly Labor Rate (HLR): Fee for services of the professional consultant(s).

◊ Hourly Rate (HR): Total rate charged per hour.

◊ Hourly Overhead Rate (HOR): Cost of expenses as part of hourly rate (HR).

◊ Hourly Profit Rate (HPR): Cost of risk as part of hourly rate (HR).

	Consultant Pay (Labor)	Business Expenses (Overhead)	Profit Margin	Total Costs
Hourly Fees	HLR	HOR	HPR	Hourly Rate (HR)
Daily Fees	DLR	DOR	DPR	Daily Rate (DR)

Notice that we are still accounting for three parts: labor, overhead, and profit. We are also providing two fee structures: one to charge by the hour, and the other to charge a per diem fee.

Calculating a Daily and Hourly Labor Rate

"Fine. But I still don't know how to set my labor rate. What should I charge as the value of my time?" One simple way to do this is to set your initial labor rate at or slightly more than you currently make in your employment (Keoughan & Joanning, 1997). If that rate is not satisfactory (you are currently unemployed or under-employed), then you can use your potential income or even your goal to establish this rate. Just be realistic. Remember from early in this chapter that fees are based on reputation and skill, among other things. If you inflate your fees, you may not get any business.

Now let's get to that example. Let's say that Ned Biggerbucks currently makes $30,000 (realistic in a small Midwestern town) and would like to move into consulting work while maintaining his salary. What should he charge? Well, first let's determine the Daily Labor Rate for Ned. Assuming that Ned will work five days a week (with 104 days off—weekends but no vacation), he will have 261 working days in a year. Dividing his salary ($30,000) by the number of working days (261) we get the following: 30,000 / 261 = $114.95 (rounded). So Ned's DLR would round to $115.

How about another example? This time we have Ed Zekutive who wants to change careers from administration in a behavioral health agency to consulting. Ed will also work five days a week. Ed's salary, however, is twice Ned's at $60,000. What would be his DLR? Remember that the DLR = Salary/Working Days. So Ed's DLR equals $60,000/261 or $229.88—rounded up to $230. No surprise for you math wizards, as his doubled salary leads to a doubled DLR.

Now it's your turn:

Work Days Calculation:

Days in a Year	365
Minus Weekends (104 days for Saturday/Sunday):	- _____
Vacation Days:	- _____
Sick Days:	- _____
Other Days (Administration etc.):	- _____
Total Work Days:	= _____
Annual proposed salary:	_____

Annual work days: _____

DLR = Salary _____ / Work Days _____

DLR = _____ Rounded up to _____

To determine an Hourly Labor Rate (HLR) you would divide the DLR by the number of hours that you consider a full day of work. For this example, let's assume this to be an eight-hour day. How does Ed Zekutive use his DLR to calculate his HLR? Simply divide the DLR by the number of hours to be worked in a day. HLR = DLR/Hours. Or $230 DLR divided by 8 hours. DLR $230/8 hours = $28.75. Rounded up, his HLR would be $30.

Is the DLR and the HLR the full cost of his services? NO! Don't forget, we still need to add overhead and a profit margin. And we may need to add *direct expenses* as well, as we'll see later. Direct expenses are costs that are incurred as part of the services on a specific consulting project. These vary by job and can include things like travel, accommodations, supplies, printing, or even additional labor. These are not the normal expenses of running the business (phone, electricity, etc.—overhead) but additional expenses as part of the consulting project itself. More on this later.

Calculating and Applying Daily and Hourly Overhead Rates

Overhead is a fee charged to all clients as a percentage of any work done to pay for the cost of running the business. Overhead is fixed expenses—costs the business has to pay no matter how much or little work is being done. This includes things like rent, telephone, postage, copying, marketing, benefits, professional fees, and the like. These expenses are established through careful planning and a budgeting process (initially through a business plan, for a start-up business).

To establish the Daily Overhead Rate (DOR) and the Hourly Overhead Rate (HOR)—which will be added to the equivalent Labor Rate—we must know two things: (1) the total overhead expenses, and (2) the number of expected days or hours billed. Notice this is days/hours *billed,* not worked. This calculation is determined by the amount of time you expect to be providing billable consulting services. If you calculate overhead based on the days worked, you will undercharge for your expenses—and perhaps put your business at serious risk.

For our example, we will use a calculation of *monthly* expenses and number of monthly billing days. However, businesses can have seasonal differences, and actual overhead rates are best determined by an annual estimate or actual expenses and billing days. We'll use the monthly example here to make it simpler, but in actually determining your own overhead rate, it is important to project it on an annual basis—as you may not bill as many days during the holiday season as you do in the spring or summer, for example.

Ed Zekutive Sample Budget
Daily Labor Rate (DLR) = $230

Item	Monthly Cost (Dollars)
Rent	600
Telephone	200
Copying/Printing	100
Postage/Shipping	60
Mileage/Travel	230
Insurance	250
Benefits	500
Professional Development	100
Office Supplies	160
Equipment	120
Accounting/Professional	150
Marketing (4 Days @ DLR of $230)	920
Other/Miscellaneous	110
Total Monthly Expenses	$3,500

To calculate the Daily Overhead Rate, this cost must be spread over the number of days billed, in this case for the month. Let's assume that Ed anticipates billing fifteen days in this month—the rest of the days he will be marketing, writing proposals, and handling other business tasks. His total monthly overhead thus equals $3,500. The number of billing days equals fifteen. Thus, the overhead cost per day is equal to the overhead divided by the billing days, or

Overhead $3,500 /15 billing days = DOR $233.33 per day.

Calculating the (Final and Total) Daily and Hourly Rate

To calculate a final Daily and Hourly rate, we add the cost of labor (DLR or HLR) to the cost of overhead (DOR or HOR) and add a percentage for profit to get the final rate. Profit margins vary across industries, and establishing a tolerable number is a factor of the items listed earlier—reputation, skill, and so on. In consulting literature percentages generally range from 16–25 percent, though some seem to demand much more!

For our example we will assume a rate of 20 percent. In practice, it is likely that you will need to adopt a figure and adjust this as time and experience increases your knowledge of the market you are operating in. For clarity, we will deal with the DR and HR separately. For calculating a Daily Rate (DR) using Ed Zekutive's figures, we have established a DLR of $230 and a DOR rate of $233.33 (or 101 percent of his Labor rate). To calculate the final rate we add

Daily Labor Rate	$230.00
Overhead (101%)	233.33
Subtotal	463.33
Profit (assume 20%)	92.67
Total	556.00
Rounded Up the Daily Rate	= $600

To calculate a final Hourly Rate (HR), take the DR and divide it by the hours worked in a billed day—here eight hours. So, the HR = DR/Hours. Or in our example: HR = DR $600/8 hours. HR = $75.

Pricing Consulting Work

Now that we have established the Daily and Hourly Rate, how do you use this to price consulting work? If you keep in mind the three components—labor, overhead, and profit—pricing consulting work becomes a straightforward process. Suppose Ed Zekutive gets a consulting contract. In his planning process he comes up with the following tasks:

Consultation Activity	Consultant Time (Days)
Meetings with Executive Staff	0.5 Days
Develop Focus Group Interview Guide	1 Day
Conduct and Evaluate Focus Groups	4 Days
Follow up and Final Report	2 Days
Total	7.5 Days

Now let's follow the formula to establish a "bottom line" cost. Assuming that Ed is a "one man shop" and he provides all the services listed, then we can apply the formula: Daily Rate (DR) x Consultant Time (Days) to establish the cost of the contract.

So using Ed's Daily Rate of $600 established previously and 7.5 days of consultant time, we come up with: $600 x 7.5 Days = $4,500 total cost. Note that because of the way the daily rate is calculated, we have accounted for the overhead and profit. What we still have *not* accounted for is any direct costs that *this* consulting project might require—this either is "eaten" if small or included as a separate cost in the contract.

> *We have created an online calculator and an Excel spreadsheet to calculate your fees. You will find them at www. hsystemsconsulting.com/ resources.php.*

A Different Approach: Value-Based Pricing

Alan Weiss (2002, 2003) has built his fees based on the value he can create for the business or organization. Weiss states that he believes it to be unethical to charge by the day or hour, as that encourages slower work and prolonging the engagement. He uses a deep understanding of business and marketing with a strong ability to negotiate to get high fees for his work.

To do this he touts his work as providing a high (or the highest?) level of service. Calls are returned promptly. Value is given through many approaches. His approach is best for those who are, or are willing to become, comfortable with an assertive bargaining mindset. It is also beneficial for those who do not come by this stance naturally, and who need to overcome what he calls the "low self-esteem" that can cause consultants to under-value and thus under-sell themselves.

Weiss's questions to establish value, and his general approach to understanding the worth of the consultant and consulting, are very beneficial, and his books are recommended reading for new or seasoned consultants.

It should be noted that while Alan Weiss appears to be very successful in his approach, he has a highly specialized background: PhD in psychology. Undergraduate work in political science. Popular author and speaker. Marketing and branding guru and human relations expert. The list goes on and on. Dr. Weiss has certainly changed the conversation of businesses and has become a force in the organizational world in generating a new paradigm for business: value.

As a skeptic, and a proponent of authenticity and fairness, I must mention that I have also begun to hear phrases like "value-added" as code for "you get a cheaper product unless you pay us more," which makes me wonder if the power of a value-based approach has lost some of its appeal—however, that could just be my own perspective. I have no problem with the idea of the customer paying more for enhanced value (which I believe is Weiss's approach)—just a concern that some will turn this approach into getting paid for the ability to provide a good "spin" on their services, a practice that I am not comfortable endorsing. With that caution in mind, we will now turn to some of the practical issues to deal with as you become a consultant.

"Rubber Meets the Road" Issues

When proposing a qualitative process, the consultant should propose a range of services and costs. There can be a "Maximum Allowed" cap on the project, but there should not be a "Minimum Required" clause, as the consultant may find a key individual or fact that may resolve the issues more quickly than anticipated—thus completing the proposal and undervaluing the consultant's work in preparing, proposing, and completing the work. If you uncover a key piece of information, or a resource that solves the problem, then you have proved your efficiency and value and should be rewarded appropriately.

A significant issue in the sales process in providing qualitative consulting is educating the client of the need (only if it exists!) for a deep understanding of the issues, participant buy-in, and achieving the desired outcomes. This helps to persuade the potential client that the consultant has correctly assessed the situation and is applying the proper framework, methods, and process to resolve the issues.

Payments should occur when the consulting activities start, as they stay on schedule, and be concluded by the time the final tasks are complete. Never work when payments are late, or without a significant portion paid when the work begins. It is not unusual to have half paid when the contact is signed and the rest paid over the course of the consulting process or at the time of the final delivery. If payments are not forthcoming, then you must cease the work and confront this problem immediately.

CHAPTER 10

Look at Me!
I'm an Entrepreneur
(I just don't know how to spell it!)
Issues in Setting Up a Consulting Practice

Choosing a Name

C hoosing a name is a daunting process. What are you trying to accomplish with the name? Are you trying to project a specific brand? Connect your specialty to you as a consultant? Make the name memorable? The decisions you make here may contribute to your ultimate success or failure.

I recently ate at a restaurant whose name consisted of two words: budget followed by the type of food. For sake of not getting sued I'll not mention its name but just imagine: Budget Pizza, Budget Salad, Budget Tacos. What does this name say to you? For me, it says one thing: cheap. As we were traveling—with sick teenagers recuperating back in the hotel room—it was our best option (and as it turned out the food was good), but we had to overcome the negative connotation to eat in their establishment.

Take your time, read several opinions about naming your business, and go back to your ideas about what services you will provide. Make a choice and ask many people what they think of when they hear the name—what brand it suggests. Then make a final choice and don't freak out. The name can always be changed later if necessary—Toyota recognized their new luxury car should not be a Toyota and created a new brand: the Lexus.

What Type of Business Form Will You Take?

Sole Proprietorship

If you have started consulting, billing, and collecting a fee without formally filing paperwork with the government to declare yourself as a business, and you own and operate the business and have all the assets in your own name, then you are operating as a sole proprietorship.

From a business standpoint, this means that all the assets and all the liabilities are yours alone. Most small businesses start out as sole proprietorships, as this is the simplest form in which to operate. However, the fact that you as the owner have personal liability for the business has made many consultants choose incorporation for some protection against litigation. Sole proprietorships can contract for labor, bill for services, collect fees—all the activities of a corporation—but the business is inseparable from you as an individual. This is very different from the forms that follow, where the business is a separate and unique entity apart from you as the owner.

Partnership

Some business owners want to set up their business with another person. This results in a partnership. Partnerships can be simple or limited liability forms. A simple partnership results when all partners are equally responsible for the liabilities and share in the assets of the company.

A limited liability partnership operates like a corporation and has the advantage of limiting the owners' liability to the amount invested in the company. Limited Liability Corporations (LLCs) have become a more popular form of business, and experts on consulting tend to be mixed in their support or lack of support for this form as viable for consultants.

If you are interested in a partnership you should ask yourself why. What advantages will this bring over a simple incorporation? What if something goes wrong? Do the advantages really outweigh the risks? A good lawyer can help you to sort out the right form of business to reach your goals. In any case, a partnership must be protected by a well-crafted agreement of some sort to protect each party.

Life changes, and partnerships are impacted by those changes. What seems true today—"he's a hard worker"— may no longer be true in five years. Often the best way is to incorporate separately: You can always have separate agreements for things you want to do together, such as a shared office agreement to allocate overhead costs.

Incorporation

An incorporated entity (Corporation) is a separate legal entity that has a legal status separate from the owner(s). They can be organized in various ways, including for-profit or nonprofit. Some states have a separate professional incorporation (see below) for those in a professional practice—doctors, therapists, dentists, and others.

The greatest advantage of incorporation is that the corporation as a separate legal entity is responsible for the liability obligations of your company. For-profit incorporation comes in two basic types, C corporations and S corporations. A discussion of the pros and cons of these types is beyond the scope of this book and can vary from state to state. Again, the way to identify the best option is through working with a lawyer in your state.

Currently the cost of the initial incorporation process runs $1,000–$1,500 in the Midwest—it may be more elsewhere. Incorporation may also create the need for an accountant to help set up the business's bookkeeping practices, generate financial documents for the corporation, and advise you on how to minimize your tax implications—this is well worth the time and investment for the business and your own family's financial planning.

Professional Licensure and Incorporation

In some states professionals have a special type of corporation that may provide some legal protection for you as a mental health provider—a lawyer can advise you on the best way to incorporate your business in your state. Consultants generally are unregulated and do not have any licensing requirements; however, any work that you do as a mental health professional may be subject to the licensing laws of your state.

The line between consulting and therapy services should be clear in your mind, but there could be activities that overlap in the mind of your clients and regulators. If any of the services you offer could be construed as providing therapy, then you must either contract in such a way to make the distinction clear or, preferably, comply with the licensing requirements in your state.

Running the Practice

Becoming a consultant yourself, if you are self-employed, means that you will be running a business. Managing projects. Possibly employing others and managing them as well. The good news is this—the fact that you are engaged in this process will only increase your knowledge and skills and, ultimately, will make you even more qualified to consult with other businesses. You will be dealing with employment taxes, accounting, expenses and revenue, accounts receivable, marketing, and other issues that every business must manage. This experience will make you more aware of and experienced in the very challenges your clients face in managing their own businesses. This increases your value as a potential partner in consulting.

Credentialing

There currently is no specific regulation of "consulting" as a profession. This is both good news and bad. On the good side, you do not have to meet some standards in order to practice. There is no ruling body to answer to or fees to pay. As a professional, you may never have to be credentialed other than in your mental health profession. However, there is bad news as well.

First, like you, no one has to meet any external standards in order to practice. Prepared or not, skilled or unskilled, educated or good at hype, nothing prevents anyone from presenting themselves as consultants. Second, there are credentials being offered, and in the future you may need these credentials to be taken seriously. If you are interested in credentialing as a consultant, then you can check out the Institute of Management Consultants USA online.

Ethics and Legal Issues

Ethical issues can be different in consulting compared to counseling. In the general consulting world, discussions would surround protecting research and development or industrial secrets. In counseling we talk about privacy and confidentiality. As mental health professionals, many consultants continue to talk in terms of confidentiality without understanding that those standards might not apply in the same way in working with organizations. Let's talk about some areas where there may be some differences.

First, identification of the client may differ from counseling. In counseling, one individual, couple, or family is considered the client. In consulting, by contrast, you may have more difficulty knowing who the client is—depending upon the situation, it could be the board/stockholders, the CEO, the organization, the employees, or the clients of the organization.

Because of this potential plethora of "clients," you must be careful to outline in the proposal/contract who the client is, including who has the power to contract and terminate the contract, who will authorize the consultant's activities, and who will get the feedback from the consultation.

Second, the concept of informed consent may differ from counseling. In counseling the idea of informed consent relates to "giving permission" for treating the client and using their personal health information. In business there is not a similar legislative protection of personal information. However, this does not mean that the consultant can be ignorant of the potential risks. This may be especially true in a coaching scenario and should be addressed formally in the contracting phase.

In consulting we need informed consent for a similar reason—the threat of harm to the individual. Some employees fear retribution or potential harm to their careers based on their participation or refusal to participate. If participation is mandatory, the consultant still has the issue of gaining trust and getting open participation.

Third, restrictions on dual relationships are quite different. In the counseling world, therapists cannot enter into business arrangements with clients, have friendships with people they treat, or be the therapist for family or friends—this is based on the idea that clients may be vulnerable to abuses and therapists' judgments may be influenced. The boundaries are addressed in ethical guidelines and are rigidly enforced.

In business there is no assumption of vulnerability on the client's part; in fact, they may be seen as peers or even in a superior position as the employer. The consultant has to consider the proper boundaries in each case and act in a professional manner, but no special limits are mandated.

Fourth, confidentiality also has some different elements. Confidentiality in a business world may be difficult or impossible to enforce. Focus groups, for instance, may prevent any guarantee of confidentiality of information. Businesses may be more concerned about proprietary information about the company or its operations being disclosed. However, in some cases (coaching or individual ethnographic interviews, for instance) confidentiality may be an important issue. Stating what and how information will be shared is critical in these instances.

Fifth, the goals are different in business than in the helping professions. In working with organizations, you must keep in mind that the goals in this environment are different than in the mental health field. Businesses exist to accomplish outcomes that are not necessarily focused on the welfare of the individual above all else. Production, profit, and survival may take precedence over the welfare of any one individual or group of individuals.

Find out more about consulting ethics at www. hsystemsconsulting.com/ resources.php.

Sixth, the scope of the work differs. In the mental health world, the therapist's scope of practice is determined by training, skill, expertise, experience, and the licensing of the state. In consulting, the scope of work is determined by these same factors, but generally is not defined by a regulating body or the state.

Branding/Marketing—How Do I Keep Supporting Myself?

Branding

In the Old West, cattle were often roaming "out on the range" and brands were used to identify ownership of individual cattle. However, brands indicated much more than mere ownership. What else did the brand signify? Well, people then were much like people today: An individual's brand signified much more than just ownership, it spoke volumes about the value of that particular animal.

Living in small towns for most of my life (8,000 people or fewer) has turned out, in retrospect, to be an interesting social experiment. In a small town—and in larger communities this is true for those "visible" families or businesses—everyone knew who they would or would not buy a car or piece of used equipment from. How? By what most would call the reputation of its owner. In the small town and in the Midwest farming country from which I hail, it is common knowledge who takes care of their equipment and who doesn't.

Among the ranchers of the past, it is easy to suppose that the animal's brand carried this same sense of value or lack of value. I can almost hear it as I watched one of the old westerns—*Bonanza, The Wild Wild West,* or *Big Valley.* "That's a Barkley brand." That meant something. In the case of the Barkleys of *Big Valley* it meant quality, value, intense protection of their rights, and benevolent dictatorship or something like it. The brand stood for much more than ownership—it increased, or in other cases decreased, the value of the product. But mostly it meant, *"Don't mess with Barkely stuff!"*

And of course we do the same thing today. How are the following items branded? Walmart. Lexus. McDonald's. Enron. Apple's iPod. Harley-Davidson. These products and many, many others have a powerful sense of branding. We may disagree on the value of each of these products based on our individual biases or experiences but, in the generalized sense of the marketplace, these products have developed a brand that stands for much more than mere ownership.

Managing the meanings or values associated with your brand is an important business function. For what do you want to be known? What values will your customers buy?

Getting Known for What You Do

Ultimately, I believe, consultants will be branded by the quality of the work and the services they provide. However, you should not leave this up to chance. Successful businesses typically have a plan for marketing themselves—you should as well. Many small business owners, especially those in the start-up phase, market in inconsistent and ineffectual ways. Therapists, for instance, who start their own practice often follow a "feast or famine" path. They market to "fill the pipeline" with clients, but as they become busy they stop. Referrals then start to dry up. As business slows, they then begin to worry and start to market once again.

Remember the research on the *Fortune 500* firms where 40 percent didn't exist after fifty years? Your "pockets" are probably not as deep as theirs were. Don't let complacency eat your business alive.

Your Unique Selling Point

What do you want to be known for? How do others see you? Why will people come to you? One approach to marketing is to focus on becoming known as *the* expert in some niche or specialty, essentially becoming synonymous with your unique traits. This is the ultimate in branding. Kleenex is facial tissue and at times actually Kleenex brand. Getting a Coke in the Midwest may actually mean a Coke but can mean a soft drink. To develop this unique selling point, it is often good to submit to the process of developing a full business plan.

While developing a business plan is not strictly necessary unless you are seeking outside capitalization (read: money), it is often a good disciplinary practice for someone starting a new venture. A business plan forces you to think through the start-up process, make decisions about what you will do as a business and how you will operate. It prompts the owner to think about the market you will be competing in and how you will attempt to sell your product—all of which are important to the lifeline of your business.

There are cheap software options for creating business plans, online tools, and books specific to consultants or coaching (Holtz, 1994; Brown-Volkman, 2003) Do yourself a favor, spend the money, time, and effort to create a business plan. You will be facing these issues and making these decisions anyway, so remember—borrowing from the history of two very different "ships"—your goal is to land on the moon not re-create the Titanic's maiden voyage.

Marketing

Experts in marketing tell us that marketing is more than selling. It incorporates the definition of services, the positioning of services relative to competitors', how services are priced and delivered, and how those services are promoted. For the sake of getting started, it is important to realize how encompassing this marketing is; however, we will focus on specific ways to promote your consulting practice.

Personality and Marketing

As a business owner you will be selling or marketing a product. As the Man in Black says in Morgenstern's *Princess Bride*, "Life is pain, Highness. Anyone who says differently is selling something."

Some of us believe that selling makes life a pain. Nevertheless, in consulting you are selling yourself and your abilities. Selling/marketing evokes different reactions from different personalities. It is an interesting challenge to some. Excitement in others. Indifference perhaps to some. Dread certainly to others.

For those in the helping professions, marketing often has meant networking rather than selling. Often we're more comfortable in a world seen as a win-win proposition than the competitive win-lose mentality of the open market. However, we are still marketing/selling. This is not a value judgment: Seeking win-win situations is, and can continue to be, a choice of successful consultants. But their marketing is likely to look very different from those who thrive on the competitive environment of a win-lose scenario.

If, as a child, you sold your tricycle, with a sizable mark-up; if you regularly turn your vacations into tax write-offs, or owned your first house by age twenty (I once met two brothers who as teenagers each owned a house out of state, near their grandparents, as an investment—and so every trip they made to see their grandparents became a tax write-off), then the following marketing approaches are probably way too passive, slow, and—dare I say it?—boring for you.

If, however, the idea of a cold call leaves you, well, cold, and "selling" (and the love of money) is akin to sitting in the seat of evil, then you need help. Help, that is, to find a way to market (and yes, sell) in a way that does not violate your principles. It is to you, those in the latter camp, that I am speaking here. The former people—the natural-born aggressive marketers—probably will want to move on to the current motivational marketing books with titles such as *The Dominating Tiger Within* and *UnleashingYour Hidden Ninja* (my apologies if these books in fact exist and are your motivating framework).

A Naturalistic Approach to Marketing

The good news for those who are not excited by the prospect of selling—whose "tiger within" is more of a house cat and whose Ninja likes to share wisdom rather than compete with steel—is that there are many effective methods that are not high pressure, cold call methods. Some selling methods include public speaking, publishing, providing pro-bono work, creating a newsletter, teaching locally, volunteering, and networking.

There are a number of resources for how to make these approaches effective. Make it part of your plan to develop a consistent approach (see my suggestions at www.hsystemsconsulting.com/resources.php). Successful consultants may spend as much as 40 percent of their time in marketing—it's that important for your sustained success.

Now Go Do It!

I had friends once who were very intelligent. It seemed that they, especially the wife, could converse on almost any topic with depth and insight. It was most impressive. However, they never seemed to do anything besides read about all these topics. She had a deep knowledge of gardening but no garden. They bought an acreage with a building, talked about growing various cash crops, but never actually bought any plants, set up the building, or started the business. It reminded me of a childhood friend who always wanted me to bring my baseball because his was starting to unravel—I wondered, *What does he plan to do with it?* (You see my cynical side started very early.)

To become a consultant, you must go out and consult. Start small. Do something that fits within your level of comfort or perhaps stretches you just a little and use this as a first step into the world of consulting. Let me know how it goes. (I promise not to make fun of any decisions about saving your baseball—I'm older and more cynical about my cynicism.) Consulting is an adventure. An adventure that can help you gain more freedom, do the work you like, and increase your income.

Appendix A:

Sample Cover/Management Letters

More examples at
www.hsystemsconsulting.com/resources.php.

Example A1: A very basic cover letter.

Human Systems Consultation, Inc.
123 Country Road
Cityville, ST 54321

Executive Director
Service Association
222 West Street
Cityville, NE 54320

January x, 20xx

RE: Consultation Proposal

Dear Director:

Attached to this letter is the proposal as discussed at our meeting on Wednesday, _____. The development of the proposal includes attention to three specific parts of the project: first, a summary of the purpose and goals of the consultation; second, a statement of the agency and consultant's roles and responsibilities; third, a proposal for engaging the undersigned as a consultant to meet the stated goals.

It is obvious from our meetings that time and effort has already been invested by the board, agency leadership, and staff in securing past funding and providing a future vision for the behavioral health services you provide. I am excited to bring my past history of success in writing grants to add to the work already done by the agency. I look forward to working with you to build on your successes and secure the needed funding. It is hoped that the time and effort reflected in the attached document will further the success of SA and the ability to create a positive future for the Behavioral Health services.

Respectfully,

Bryan G. Miller, Ph.D.

Bryan G. Miller, Ph.D.

Consultant

Sample A2: A little more complex letter.

Human Systems Consultation, Inc.
123 Country Road
Cityville, ST 54321

Local Church Leadership
333 Avenue Ave.
Metro, NE 65421

January x, 20xx

RE: Consultation Proposal

Dear Leadership Team Members:

Attached to this letter are the items discussed at our meeting on Monday, January 28, 20xx. This includes three specific parts: first, a summary of the consultant's understanding of the current situation and general impressions of the aforementioned meeting; second, a proposal for engaging the undersigned as a consultant to meet the Leadership Team's goals; and third, a "thumbnail" of the proposed consultant's involvement—which may be edited by the Team in accordance with their understanding of the planning that has been completed—and included in the overall presentation to the congregation.

As you are aware, the urgency of the presentation to the congregation led to an emphasis on discussing the Team's current situation and the crafting of an agreement on how to proceed, without a discussion of the Leadership's perceptions of the consultant's involvement with the congregation; therefore, the proposal is presented as the first step in a dialogue to craft the recommended actions to achieve the session's stated goals. It is deemed presumptuous to propose specific remedies/actions to take until the nature of the congregational need and involvement is understood.

One of the reasons for hiring a family therapist, as was recommended to the Leadership Team, is the framework this profession adopts, which views families or organizations as a "system" rather than a collection of individuals. Thus, "the whole is more than the sum of its parts," and a system (such as an elephant) cannot be divided into separate parts (dividing an elephant does not produce two smaller elephants!). From a systems perspective, this diversion—from specifically discussing the consultant's role to the immediate decisions of the Team—was necessary, as actions by one part of the system necessarily are interdependent with and affect the other parts of the system. The Team's decision on how to present the proposed plan to the congregation therefore is critical in its impact on any work with the congregation and will influence the congregation's ability to engage and carry out current and future plans.

It is obvious that much time and effort has already been invested by the Leadership Team and the Overseeing Committee in trying to craft a positive future for the Local Church. That future appeared to be in jeopardy and continues to be critical to any work that is to be accomplished with the congregation. It is hoped that the time and effort reflected in the attached document will further your work and the ability to create a positive future for the Church.

Respectfully,

Bryan G. Miller, Ph.D.

Bryan G. Miller, Ph.D.

Consultant

Appendix B:

Sample Proposals

More examples at
www.hsystemsconsulting.com/resources.php.

Example B1: A simple proposal.

Human Systems Consultation, Inc.
Consultation Proposal

March 13, 20xx

Business Consult
Proposal

Purpose
To assist the Department, managers and employees, in developing productive working relationships and action plans to reach top performance as a group.

Rationale
Just as top athletes and performers employ vocal coaches, sports psychologists, performance consultants, etc., managers often employ consultants to help achieve top performance in their industry.

Work teams are frequently at the heart of these businesses. These teams, like the organizations that house them, can benefit from the use of consultants to aid them in moving to even higher levels of achievement and satisfaction.

The consultant brings an outsider's perspective, combined with experience with other teams and industries, tools and resources, and extra time and energy, to act as a catalyst to help teams achieve their top performance.

For the _____ team, an understanding of the dynamics of working with teammates with different personality styles and implementing those strengths into specific targeted action plans for addressing core issues will be implemented.

Services as proposed include:

Assessment and Planning:

Meeting with Coordinator	0.5 hour
Review HR interview data	1 hour
Meeting with HR representative	0.5 hour
Proposal development	3 hours

Meeting with Coordinator & HR to review & revise
proposal as necessary and pre-plan targeted areas
for Team meeting   2 hours

Implementation:

Team completes Myers-Briggs Type Instrument,
reviews personality types of team and the
relationship to team performance   3 hours

Team meeting (employees, management & HR)
to develop specific action plans to address
core issues   4 hours

Follow-up meeting with managers & HR
to review action plans, target dates,
evaluation of achievement   1 hour

Presentation of finalized action plans
and commitment to change with team members   2 hours

Follow-Up Meeting with HR representative
and managers to assess implementation progress   1 hour

Total   **18 hours**

Project Costs

Cost of Consultant Services:

Assessment and Planning:

Meeting with Coordinator	No Charge
Review HR interview data	No Charge
Meeting with HR representative	No Charge
Proposal development	$$$

Meeting with Coordinator & HR to review & revise proposal as necessary and pre-plan targeted areas for team meeting $$$

Implementation:

Team completes Myers-Briggs Type Instrument,*reviews personality types of team and the relationship to team performance $$$

Team meeting (employees, management & HR) to develop specific action plans to address core issues $$$

Follow-up meeting with managers & HR to review action plans, target dates, evaluation of achievement $$

Presentation of finalized action plans and commitment to change with team members $$$

Follow-Up

Meeting with HR representative and managers to assess implementation progress $$

Total Cost $$$$

*Consultant may bill for significant direct costs related to this project in addition to the amount listed above as pre-approved by the agency. This may include but is not limited to MBTI instruments ($10 per person est.), printing, excessive mileage, additional consultation hours, etc.

Consult Timeline

Week of:	March	6	13	20	27	April	3	10	17	24	May	June
Meeting with Coordinator		*										
Review HR interview data		*										
Meeting with HR representative for preliminary proposal		*										
Proposal development		*										
Meeting with Coordinator & HR to review & revise proposal and pre-plan targeted areas for team meeting		*	*	*								
Completion of MBTI, review personality types of team and the relationship to team performance					*							
Team meeting (employees, management & HR) to develop specific action plans to address core issues							*	*				
Follow-up meeting with managers & HR to review action plans, target dates, evaluation of achievement								*	*			
Presentation of finalized action plans and commitment to change with team members.									*	*		
Meeting with HR representative and managers to assess implementation progress											*	*

Sample B2:
A proposal addressing church conflict.

Human Systems Consultation, Inc.
123 Country Road
Cityville, ST 54321

Local Leadership Team
444 Street
Metro, NE 98765

RE: Consultation Proposal

Dear Team Members:

Attached to this letter are the items discussed at the meeting on Monday, _____. This includes three specific parts; first, a summary of the consultant's understanding of the current situation and general impressions of the aforementioned meeting; second, a proposal for engaging the undersigned as a consultant to meet the Leadership Team's goals; and third, a "thumbnail" of the proposed consultant's involvement— which may be edited by the Team in accordance with their understanding of the planning that has been completed— and included in the overall presentation to the congregation.

As you are aware, the urgency of the presentation to the congregation led to an emphasis on discussing the Team's current situation and the crafting of an agreement on how to proceed, without a discussion of the Team's perceptions of the consultant's involvement with the congregation; therefore, the proposal is presented as the first step in a dialogue to craft the recommended actions to achieve the Team's stated goals. It is deemed presumptuous to propose specific remedies/actions to take until the nature of the congregational need and involvement is understood.

One of the reasons for hiring a family therapist, as was recommended to the Team, is the framework this profession adopts which views families or organizations as a "system" rather than a collection of individuals. Thus "the whole is more than the sum of its parts" and a system (such as an elephant) cannot be divided into separate parts (dividing an elephant does not produce two smaller elephants!). From a systems perspective, this diversion—from specifically discussing the consultant's role to the immediate decisions of the Team—was necessary as actions by one part of the system necessarily are interdependent with and affect the other parts of the system. The Team's decision on how to present the proposed plan to the congregation therefore is critical in the impact on any work with the congregation and will influence the congregation's ability to engage and carry out current and future plans.

It is obvious that much time and effort has already been invested by the Team and the Governing Body in trying to craft a positive future for Local Church. That future appeared to be in jeopardy and continues to be critical to any work that is to be accomplished with the congregation. It is hoped that the time and effort reflected in the following document will further your work and the ability to create a positive future for the Church.

Respectfully,
Bryan G. Miller, Ph.D.
Bryan G. Miller, Ph.D.
Consultant

Observations and Reflections on Leadership Team Meeting January ___, 20xx

General Observations:

◊ Due to past history, both positive and negative (a long-term pastoral relationship vs. the discipline and resignation of a program leader) there is significant and long-standing disagreement among Team members themselves and within the congregation over the future direction of leadership of the church. This disagreement, despite much effort to find a positive future, continues and includes in it the current plan to engage in a six-month process of Ministerial Agreement.

◊ This dissention may have been compounded by engaging in the difficult task of starting an organizational/cultural change process concurrently with the events listed above.

◊ In spite of the disagreements that exist, there seems to be a genuine concern among Team members for the church, which expresses itself in the passion of this disagreement. This was reflected in the concern and burden Team members expressed, as well as their behavior as indicated in the next few bullet points.

◊ Members of the Team are able to speak honestly and openly about these disagreements and maintain respect for those with opposite viewpoints. Team members appeared genuinely grieved about the current impact on the church, seem to fear for its future, and to express a positive view of the church and its members in general.

◊ Pastor Johnson specifically, and Team members generally, are able to admit to mistakes made in the past, verbally commit to changes in the future, and accept and discuss these without reacting, in the most part, with a defensive response.

◊ Some specific and tangible changes have to be made. The church itself appears ripe for further dissention and conflict if decisive action is not taken by leadership. The urgency of this is underscored by the recent resignations of some Leaders, the prepared proposal for the dissolution of the pastor's call (read, but not presented as a motion in the Team meeting), and the Team's concerns over a potential call by some in the congregation for a vote on dissolution of the pastor's call in the near future.

◊ The risks of an unplanned, conflict-driven resolution to these issues are significant. The possibility of serious damage to the church as it exists and its members is very high and the Team acknowledges this reality.

◊ The current plan for a Ministry Agreement to address the three areas of the pastoral role, the Team's operations, and the congregation's involvement has support only if it leads to change and the cessation of the current conflict. While Team members appear to be concerned with the welfare of the church, there are varying degrees of confidence in the ability to achieve significant change.

◊ Accordingly, it appears necessary to commit to a significant decision point, at six months, when the Team can act on its leadership role to decide if sufficient change has occurred or if a resignation or dissolution of call is required.

◊ The Congregational Covenant portion of the plan was not discussed specifically, nor the specific involvement of the Consultant in this process; however, its success will be directly related to the ability of individuals to carry out the other two Covenants in Ministry.

◊ The success or failure of this agreement is dependent upon several factors:

- Those involved, both Team members and congregants, must want the plan to succeed.

- Individuals involved must learn how to work through conflict, including taking on a personal commitment to forgiveness and loving one another.

- Adequate attention to any future conflicts must be timely and not delayed.

- Expectations must be clear, realistic, and precisely defined.

- Realization that conflict is not, itself, unhealthy; that intrapersonal or interpersonal conflict involves emotional elements and must be attended to in the process of resolution of conflict.

- Members must recognize the strengths of members different than themselves (1 Cor. 12:12-20) and value those as gifts differing to build up the church—this especially applies to leadership and their support of each other in their ministry.

◊ In times of conflict it is common to seek a quick fix. Once this has failed, there is the possibility of extended conflict and the pressure or "fatigue factor" to push individuals toward blame as an "obvious reason" for taking decisive—and often traumatic— action. To engage the conflict and make often-painful and sacrificial change is much more difficult. As a consultant—although the situation is quite dire—I see the seeds of being able to take this more difficult road within the Team members, as each appears to be committed, honest in their opinions, and non-defensive. I pray that others have this same ability to allow for the leadership to define the future course for the church. There is biblical precedent for conflict that results in the furthering of God's plans, as well as reconciliation of that conflict, in the example of Paul and Barnabas (Acts 15:36-41; 2 Tim. 4:11; Gal. 2:11-14).

Consultation Proposal for Local Church

Purpose:

Local Church was formed by the merger of three churches. The former pastor served the church for twenty-seven years, after which the current pastor was called, and the church's focus became one of growth. To that end, the pastor and Team began the process of cultural transformation from being a "pastoral-focused" church to a "program-focused" one. Events since the change in pastors, and particularly in the last year, have led to significant conflict among the leadership as well as some in the congregation.

This conflict has led to several actions, including, from memory, an evaluation of the pastor's performance and some subsequent training, activation of the Governing Body's Committee (GBC) to assist the Team, and the development of a Ministerial Agreement to address three areas: the pastor's role, the functions of the Leadership Team, and the inclusion of the congregation in the change process.

The consultant was contacted by a member of the GBC of the Midland States Denomination to attend a meeting with the Team of the Local Church upon the recommendation to include a family systems specialist in its planning for a Covenant in Ministry to address conflict occurring in the church and among its leadership.

Needs:

The needs of the Team and involvement with the congregation were to be explored in collaboration with the Team and GBC representative at the meeting to be held on Monday, January 26, 20xx. The meeting resulted in the focus on some immediate clarifications and actions prompted by sensitive and critical developments that could potentially derail an intervention process. Thus the conversation regarding the goals and objectives for the consultant's role was usurped by the immediate demands of the situation. The following represents the consultant's ideas regarding interventions that would increase the probability of the Team to successfully lead the congregation to a successful decision and process for change. They are subject to further revision in collaboration with the Team.

Goals and Objectives

The following is a tentative outline of the consultation process as understood after the initial meeting with the Team and GBC. It is anticipated that this will be altered as the discussion of the plans and desired outcomes are solidified. Since specifics of the consultant's involvement were not discussed, all proposed actions are subject to revision.

From a systems model, the consultant must understand the interrelatedness of the parts and be respectful of how change in one part of the system will "reverberate" across the system causing further changes. From an organizational perspective, it is commonly understood that leadership affects those governed, and the governed influence leadership. Thus the interactions and communication of Team members, between the Team and the congregation, and among the congregation members are interdependent and richly cross-joined. Impact in any one of these spheres has the ability to impact the others and any one sphere can nullify the attempted changes by the others.

As such, it is this consultant's opinion that assuming a role of "working with the congregation" alone will be insufficient to bring about the changes necessary for success. This is not to say that the consultant must be directly involved in each activity. Other resources (such as further involvement by the GBC for instance) may take on these tasks, but the consultant must have the freedom to engage the system in a meaningful way to be effective. *If this level of involvement is not deemed agreeable for the role of the outside consultant, then a different course of action or referral to another consultant is appropriate.* If, however, there is the will, commitment, and resources to intervene meaningfully into this system, then the following broad goals would be appropriate:

1. Facilitate the Team's ability to communicate clearly its expectations (for itself, the pastor, and the congregation) initially and continuing through the six-month Covenant in Ministry process.

2. Assist the leadership in re-establishing relationships and trust in those relationships to build commitment for the six-month Ministry Agreement and for the decision to continue the change process

or move for a Dissolution of Call after the six-month period.

3.   Develop a plan for communication and involvement of the congregation (to be defined with the Team) in the Congregational Agreement process to facilitate healing and commitment to follow the Team's leadership.

4.   Assist in evaluating the degree of changes at the end of the six-month period and implementing decisions regarding continuation of the Ministry Agreement or dissolution of the pastoral call.

To accomplish this, the following activities are proposed:

◊ Meeting regularly with the Team over the next six months to facilitate communication as described above. Special focus will be on, first, developing a plan for the involvement of the Congregation in the Ministry Agreement and facilitating communication. Second, making sure that the "covert is overt" or that the Team is having honest and frank conversations about their expectations and achievement toward change, or lack of change. Third, identifying "points of intervention" for the consultant to assist in the healing process through individual or joint interviews/coaching.

◊ Individual/joint interviews at the discretion of the consultant with "key players" to promote support for the Ministry Agreement and to support open communication to and between the congregation and the Team.

◊ Once a plan for the Congregational Agreement is formulated, the consultant will actively participate in assisting in the communication, feedback, and evaluation processes as designed in collaboration with the Team.

◊ Meet with the Team and GBC periodically (to be defined by mutual agreement) throughout the six-month period, and at the end of six months to evaluate progress or lack of progress and make appropriate decisions.

Tentative Timeline:

	January	February	March	April	May	June	July
Meeting w/ Team & GBC	*						
Proposal Development	*						
Development of Goals for Congregational Agreement		*					
Meetings with Team		*	*	*	*	*	*
Individual/Joint Coaching	*	*	*	*	*		
Congregational Intervention		*	*	*	*	*	
Evaluation of Progress			*	*	*		
Facilitate Final Evaluation & Decision							*

Expected Results:

◊ A rigorous implementation of the Ministry Agreement in each of the three areas identified

◊ Development and implementation of the Ministry Agreement with the congregation

◊ Improved communication process among Team members and among other "key individuals"

◊ Improved communication between Team and congregation

◊ Participation along with the Team and GBC in evaluating the results of the progress in each area covered by the Ministry Agreement

Reporting:

Reports and findings will be delivered (as defined by the needs of the Team) through regular meetings with the Team as indicated in the timeline above. Decisions will be made by the Team and included as per their normal tradition in the notes for formal Team meetings. No formal report will be given by the consultant unless so directed by the Team.

Pricing/Contracting:

Fees will be assessed on a Fixed Fee plus Expenses basis. The Team, upon agreement with this contract/proposal, will pay Human Systems Consultation, Inc. $___ per hour for the consultant's time, to be paid monthly, with the final payment due by the end of July, 20xx. The Team will also be charged for reasonable expenses such as mileage, copying, etc., as approved by the Team. The following items/charges are offered as an example and may not reflect the actual expenses of the project.

Item	Time	Cost
Meeting w/ Team & GBC	3 Hours	No Charge
Proposal Development	5 Hours	No Charge
Development of Goals for Congregational Agreement	3 Hours	$___
Meetings with Team	12 Hours	$_____
Individual/Joint Coaching	6 Hours	$___
Congregational Intervention	6 Hours	$___
Evaluation of Progress	4 Hours	$___
Facilitate Final Evaluation & Decision	2 Hours	$___
Total Consultant Cost	41 Hours	$_____*

*Does not include any direct costs. Upon acceptance, or revision and acceptance, of this proposal, a final version to be signed as a contractual agreement will be drafted with appropriate signatures and assurances.

Resources:

Managing Church Conflict, Group Theory Applied to the Church Family. Jones, James A.; Q Books: Abilene, Texas. ISBN: 0-89137-558-9.

The Fifth Discipline: The Art and Practice of the Learning Organization. Senge, P. Doubleday: New York. ISBN: 0-385-26095-4.

The Fifth Discipline Fieldbook. Senge, P. Doubleday: New York. ISBN: 0-385-47256-0.

Working with You is Killing Me. Crowley, K. and Elster, K. Warner Books: New York. ISBN 0-446-57674-3.

Changing Human Systems. Capelle, R. International Human Systems: Toronto, Canada. ISBN: 0-9790171-1-1.

The Shaping of Things to Come. Frost, M. and Hirsch, A. Hendrickson Publishers: Peabody, MA. ISBN: 1-8768-2587-1.

Thumbnail Introduction
(Requested by Client)

At the recommendation of Dr. Tom Pelini, consulting psychologist, the Team has retained an outside consultant, Human Systems Consultation, Inc., to assist in developing and implementing a process for the inclusion of the congregation in the Covenant in Ministry. The consultant, Dr. Bryan Miller, has experience working with organizations both in his experience as an administrator and as a consultant. Dr. Miller has met with the Team and will be involved in developing the process for involving the congregation over the next few months.

About the Consultant:

Dr. Bryan G. Miller is the President of Human Systems Consulting, Inc. Dr. Miller has worked as a clinician, professor, researcher, and administrator since 1989. He has been married to Amy since 1981 and is blessed with six children.

Dr. Miller's experience has included working with family systems as the primary therapist in a children's psychiatric hospital, residential programs, school-based programs, and in outpatient settings. In 1998, as a graduate student, Dr. Miller began to apply his experience in administration and as a "systems therapist" to organizations. This led to a second career consulting with organizations and businesses. Dr. Miller has supervised and administered family-based programs and consulted with organizations for more than ten years.

Currently, Dr. Miller's work encompasses three areas. He works as a Human Systems Consultant to businesses and organizations, as an Associate Professor with Amridge University of Montgomery, Alabama, and maintains a limited private practice with the Behavioral Pediatric and Family Therapy Program in Lincoln, Nebraska.

Bryan is also the "adoptive" father of three geese, one duck, thirty to forty chickens, six cats, one dog, one horse, and forty to fifty thousand bees—as of last count.

Consultation with Local Organizations:

Some of the local organizations to whom Dr. Miller has provided consultation:

Child Center
Child Food Program – Federal Program
Service Association
First Church
Church of Midlands
Medical Partnership
Parochial Services
Second Church
St. Methodist Church
University Bank
Very Good Manufacturing
Women's Program—Federal Program

Sample B3: Yet more complex.

Preliminary Proposal
For Midwest Manufacturing

Statement of Problem

Based on observation and interviews with various personnel during our tour, the following is a preliminary description of problems which were identified from this information. From this data, the following working hypothesis has been formulated.

Several personnel stated that it has become more difficult for communication to flow effectively. Although there is a benefit in being able to micro-manage manufacturing specific products by having individual plants, it has also been a detriment causing communication to break down. Communication from [the owners and senior executives] to the Division Managers is constant and appears effective. However, once communication flows to the Plant Managers and especially to Area Supervisors several problems begin to surface.

The Plant Managers appear to be inundated with regulatory duties, deadlines, paperwork, and responsibility to manage production. The Plant Managers are in a pivotal position. On one hand, they are trying to be responsive to corporate office by meeting the deadlines for products to be manufactured and to maintain certain standards during the manufacturing process. On the other hand, they have little time for direct personal interaction with staff and

Area Supervisors. Consequently, the process of information dissemination and personal interaction can break down at this point.

The Area Supervisors also feel the burden and responsibility to produce and insure that the Plant Managers' requests are met. Depending upon the Area Supervisor, this could become an overwhelming task for several reasons. First, the majority of Area Supervisors have been promoted to their position from the floor or from them having been Leadmen. Although their knowledge and skills in production may be adequate, they may not possess skills in management of people and communication of information for the purpose of production and team building.

Secondly, under such pressure an Area Supervisor could respond with resistance toward the Plant Managers and the demands of corporate office by setting a poor or negative tone and attitude for the floor staff. While trying to placate or discredit the Plant Managers, they may attempt to recruit loyalty from the floor staff thus hindering the flow of communication. This may also hinder the team building process which is needed in order for production to be collaborative. Or, they may react in a rigid or controlling manner to the floor staff to insure that they meet the demands and quotas of their Plant Manager. This process may impinge upon their personal abilities to actually meet those demands.

Third, when "errors" of production take place (i.e., waste of material due to errors or carelessness), there may be, or is, an effort to "cover up" or minimize the problem. Therefore, the flow of communication up to the Plant Managers may not always include everything that is actually happening on the floor. Loyalty produces camaraderie especially when it means covering up your mistakes.

As you can envision, the dynamics of the "chain reaction" both up and down the hierarchy begins to impede the communication process. Whenever a person disagrees with the information being passed on there may be the inclusion of their own personal bias, attitude and possibly their own agenda. This process may be subtle, but it is most definitely influential.

Objectives and Major Considerations

Our objectives stem from our working hypothesis mentioned above and is modified from continuous information that is gathered during the formal process of inquiry. The objectives and major considerations based upon our working hypothesis are as follows:

◊ Improve floor staff efficiency and productivity through improved communication and sense of job ownership.

◊ Improve job satisfaction and performance for Plant Managers, Area Supervisors, and Floor Staff.

◊ Increase effective flow of communication up and down through identification of obstacles preventing direct communication.

◊ Identify and improve weak links in flow of communication and managerial abilities.

◊ Improved total quality management for relevant positions.

◊ Develop organization plan which enhances efficiency and interpersonal functioning.

◊ Support current Human Resource efforts and interventions for improvement.

Method & Options

Our process will include three major aspects: Assessment, Intervention, and Evaluation/Follow-up.

Assessment: The assessment phase is critical to helping us understand the corporate culture and how the organizational system of the corporation interacts with the corporate culture. Once we begin to understand the organizational system, we can then determine the problems inherent to the system, e.g., the flow of communication, excessive waste, employee dissatisfaction, or other problems which we have not yet uncovered. This process is continuous and shapes the rest of the planning and implementation. The assessment phase will include the following procedures:

1. Attend ISR's presentation of results to senior management.

2. Meet with ISR staff to review details of survey data.

3. Conduct focus groups and analyze data.

4. Provide leadership with completed action plans for ISR data and summary of qualitative analysis of focus group data.

We would be pleased to provide our services in connection with the above to _____ Company on a fixed fee basis. Listed below is our estimate of the hours that we anticipate are required on our part to complete the above activities. Please find the fixed fee that would be charged for the completion of each activity.

1. Planning:

Estimated number of hours	15-20
Fixed-fee charge	$,$$$

2. Implementing:

Estimated number of hours	65-75
Fixed-fee charge	$,$$$

3. Analysis:

Estimated number of hours	32-42
Fixed-fee charge	$,$$$

4. Reporting:

Estimated number of hours	24-34
Fixed-fee charge	$,$$$
Total amount for services:	$$,$$$

Based on the proposal outlined above, and accounting for the company's participation in the identification and notification of participants and copying of final reports, the cost of the project is understood to be $$,$$$.

We hope that the above information is sufficient to meet your requirements. If we may provide further information, please do not hesitate to let us know. We look forward to working with you on this very challenging and necessary project.

Regards,

Matthew J. Burch   Bryan G. Miller

Consultant   Consultant

Appendix C:

Sample Data Collection Instruments

_____

More examples at
www.hsystemsconsulting.com/resources.php.

Sample C1: Transcript of Interviews/ Plant Tour for Qualitative Assessment

Transcript Interviews and Plant Tour

2-13-97

Present: Two Primary Consultants

Discussion regarding December 5th walk-through of the Corporate Office

and the Plants. Persons present during walk-through on Dec. 5th: H.J.; P.J., B.M.; and

M.B. (Consultants), and Dick (Company X employee).

Spent two hours talking in conference room prior to tour and lunch. Spent entire day till

5:00 p.m. on tour.

Discussion:

Began with question directed toward Dick: "What is it like to work at the company?"

◊ Dick wanted to give us what we needed, was not sure how he was going to fill our time all day. (Seemed nervous.)

◊ Discussed his history at the company: worked for the company 29 years. Started on the floor, worked his way up to Plant Manager, now a Corporate Administrator for Bill and Mary.

◊ Gave history how the company got started, etc.

◊ H.J. discussed purpose of our study. Introduced question: "How does communication flow?"

◊ Dick stated that it has become more difficult for communication to flow easily; became more difficult once separate plants were established. Communication less effective. (Area to be explored further.)

◊ Stated communication good from Bill and Mary to Division Managers and Plant Managers. Once communication gets to area supervisors, communication breaks down, especially once it hits the floor. (Reinforced by what Kirk stated: limited amount of interaction with communication among Plant Managers. This process needs to be explored with an eye toward improving process. Plant Managers are burdened with regulatory duties, heavy paperwork loads, and have little time for direct personal interaction with staff and Plant Managers. Need to find out what kinds of meetings are taking place, their frequency, content and process, how useful or productive for people involved, are they wasting time or saving time?)

◊ Dick was very positive about flow of communication between Bill/Mary and upper levels of managers. 1. Bill/Mary have monthly meetings with Divisional Managers. 2. Bill/Mary have an open door policy with line staff. (Need to look into this. This could lead to a type of triangulation process which could undermine the flow of information). The solution needs to bring people together. A Consultant facilitator to be an advocate for the system at large? 3. There are meetings that are open to floor staff to attend (question this).

◊ Breakdown in communication between Plant Managers and Area Supervisors.

◊ Breakdown not a universal problem but a specific problem having to do with Plant Managers and Area Supervisors. (Look at what some plants are doing well and what others are not doing. Is it transferable? Is it systemic or specific to an individual? If non-systemic what is it? In addition, how much training goes into Lead persons? How much team development takes place with line staff and lead management? Is there management training for the Area and Plant Supervisors?)

◊ Dick stated that there were line staff who like to complain and Area Supervisors who have poor communication, management and social skills.

◊ Asked Dick question regarding standards of reporting waste of material compared with product manufactured. Dick said that the company could not get an accurate estimate due to Area Supervisors not wanting to divulge of the possible waste. Company therefore does not know exactly how much waste is going out. (What does this reflect? Look into this further. Ask for examples to illustrate problem. Look into quality management. Area Supervisors operating out of fear. Cannot trust their superiors to work with them and not devalue them?)

◊ Spoke to Leo (Plant Manager); stated too much to do. Not able to be on floor enough.

- Hierarchy: Division Manager
Plant Manager
Area Supervisor
Lead man (group leader)
Floor (Line staff)

◊ Certain plants were very noisy, dirty, poor air quality, poor lighting. (Does this decrease staff morale? What are the long- and short-term goals to address this?)

◊ General Observations

◊ People were working by themselves or in groups of two.

◊ How do floor people view management in the offices (castles)?

◊ People seemed comfortable to stop and chat.

◊ Noticed a significant difference between Plant 5 & 6. Elite vs. Scrub. How does the floor staff perceive the difference? If you had the choice, where would you like to be?

◊ How does management communicate the importance of product being made to the floor staff?

◊ Dick has personal ownership of the Co. To the point if he does not like decision made he still would follow through. The Co. has developed in him a loyalty and trust and ownership of his job. How did this happen?

◊ Dick is an important link—his style, his approach to cultivate Co. moral, loyalty, increase communication. His means to the Co.'s ends are helpful. Are there others in the organization like this?

◊ Leo's story about being busy and forgetting the turkey
   is important.

◊ Is there among the employees a distinction and
   division between Corporate Office and the Floor? Is
   there hostility, open or passive?

◊ Kirk—V.P. of H.R. Careful not to step on any toes.
   Politically astute. Is there a risk for him? He is eager,
   enthusiastic, perhaps not sure what he is dealing
   with. (Make sure put in letter that Kirk has ideas, be
   supportive.)

Developing a Working Hypothesis

◊ Middle management caught in a bind to satisfy line
   staff and keep upper management happy. Either they
   will discredit upper management or make it difficult
   for floor staff by being authoritarian, rigid, controlling.

◊ Systemic Hypothesis: Middle-Area Supervisors?
   Plant Managers in a precarious position/bind in that
   if they choose to stay in good relation with upper-
   management they need to put pressure on the line
   staff to be productive and meet expectations of upper
   management as translated by middle management.
   If, on the other hand, they try to please the line staff,
   who are likely to complain about wishes of upper
   management, they (middle) have to discredit upper
   management. ("They made me do this to you.")

◊ This is more likely to happen if communication, i.e.,
   flow of information both up/down in the hierarchy is

limited or of poor quality (poorly translated from one level to another).

◊ Solution to the dilemma: increase both quality and quantity of information communicated up/down the hierarchy.

◊ Goal can be accomplished through training all levels of management to communicate effectively esp. Areas of careful listening and accurate information translation.

◊ Good listening = what is said is understood and acknowledged, not just heard.

◊ When information is passed on if person disagrees with the information, the person will include their personal biases, attitudes, opinions, sentiments which decrease the accuracy of information being sent on to the next level. This contaminates information. Non-verbals are also included as a bias, i.e., tone of voice, gestures, postures, emphasis on particular words.

◊ In short, this process may be subtle, but highly influential.

◊ Check into what types of messages, information, etc., gets passed on. Try to develop an example of a message that gets contaminated.

1. Next meeting: Meet with Bill, Mary, and Kirk. Have a preliminary proposal.

2. Develop a letter: include a systemic Hypothesis. Get together and discuss this with them.

3. At the meeting decide what the next step would be

4. Systemic Hypothesis moves towards an Organizational model.

5. Next meeting will develop the plan of action.

Sample C2: Organizing Focus Group Problem Statements and Solutions

Area: Supervision

Problem Statements

1. Supervisors are not perceived as competent in technical aspects because of a lack of training about production, poor management skills (including organizational skills, strategic ability, setting daily work priorities for their area), unclear/unfocused expectations of job/project responsibilities, and non-promotion of qualified employees.

Solutions

1. Train new hires and transfers (below Plant Manager level) for a two-week period on the floor prior to taking supervisory position. Train supervisors in the areas of technical aspects of position, management/ organizational skills, project priority setting, and people skills. Establish policy to make training universal and mandatory across the board.

2. Rewrite/define job descriptions of supervisors to coincide with the different levels of technical difficulty they will supervise.

3. Rewrite job postings to encourage people with the technical experience, although they may not have a formal degree.

4. Do not require production quotas for new supervisors (criticals) for a 90-day period of time.

Problem Statements

1. Supervisors are not available when needed because they are absent from the work area due to multiple job responsibilities and/or the lack of clarity about who needs to be available and has the authority to make decisions (especially 2nd & 3rd shifts).

Solutions

1. Develop a plan where supervisors are available (emphasizing the first and last two hours) and accessible during the shift for decision-making about production.

2. Require supervisors to be in their work area or communicate where they are at all times so that they can be reached by anyone in the chain of command.

3. Define and standardize supervisor's responsibilities, titles, job descriptions, and level of authority, so that it is clear to the employees what decisions they can make (at all levels).

4. Define and increase 2nd & 3rd shifts (i.e., leadmen or leadwomen) decision-making ability due to not having area supervisors, foreman, and plant manager.

Area: Employee Involvement

Problem Statements

1. Supervisors do not involve employees in the production process (including planning their work, solving problems and making decisions) because there is poor communication between supervisors and employees. This poor communication occurs due to: a) a lack of availability of the supervisor, b) uncertainty about how decisions should be made/ problems solved, c) and supervisors not appearing to care about problems.

Solutions

1. Communicate specific customer complaints (internal and external) to the employees. Include comments—related to the specific product of the plant or line and including both positive and negative comments — to employees in the morning start-up meeting.

2. Authorize group leaders to go to manufacturing engineer to solve problems regarding production (especially 2nd and 3rd shift) to solve problems on the line.

Sample C3: Structured or Semi-Structured Interview Guide

Interviewee: _____

Date of Interview: _____

Interviewer: _____

Before we begin, please take a moment to reflect on your experiences both with this company and other companies you have worked for in the past. The management wants to understand how your experiences with the company compare to other experiences you have had with other companies, how your experience has changed, if any, over the course of your employment with this company, and what you would like to see change or stay the same in the future. Remember, all information will be shared in aggregate form and management will not have access to specific individual's responses.

In order to understand how your responses compare to others in the company, please provide the following basic information about your experience:

1. How long have you worked for the company? (Record years, then months)

2. What is your job function? (Identify employee, mid-management, senior management)

3. Who is your supervisor(s)? (Name and Title)

4. What shift do you work? (1st, 2nd, 3rd, Swing, Other)

5. What plant are you working in presently? (1-9, Office pool)

6. Have you worked in other plants for the company? Which one(s)? (Record plant number and dates)

7. What has been your experience working for other companies? (Record number of other companies, type—agricultural, manufacturing or other)

8. In general, what is the best thing about working for this company?

9. What is the worst thing about working for this company?

10. How likely are you to still be employed by the company two years from now?

11. What is the most pressing need for employees at this time?

12. What is the most pressing need for the company at this time?

Sample C4: Focus Group Guide

Bank Consultation—Loan Servicing Group
Bryan G. Miller, Ph.D.

Introduction:
Introduce consultants

◊ provide EAP and consulting services for Bank and Others

◊ consulted with Bank on more then 6 occasions in 2005

◊ provide individual counseling for employees and their families

Reason for this particular consultation

◊ Bank's high regard for employees

◊ Concerns from HR about "hearing" and acting on feedback

◊ Management's openness to feedback and action

◊ Data reviewed to date

◊ HR questionnaire and one-on-one interview summary

◊ Meeting with HR representative to gather feedback

◊ Meeting with Management to gather management views

◊ Now meeting to hear your views and begin to develop solutions

Goals/Activities for today's group

1. Identify key issues related to problem areas (may be same or different than questionnaire topics) NO CONSENSUS NEEDED TO INCLUDE

2. Identify proposed solutions to each issue (50% agreement to include) or identify past successes (no consensus) in resolving key issues

3. Rank order (prioritize) solutions as suggestions to management

Other issues

Confidentiality—reporting only aggregate data no identifiers

Taping and transcripts

Breaks

Being "called out" by Supervisor

Snacks and stretch breaks

Rules for the group

1. Respect for all members/views

2. All information is important—even minority views (custodian & stairs)

3. If necessary to refer to a particular job function use job titles not personal names

Have group members give first names and positions

Ask Grand Tour Question, "What if anything keeps this team from reaching its top performance?"

Appendix D:

Sample Reports

Sample D1:
Work Team Focus Group Results

Overall, the Bank Team identified issues of Trust, Respect, and Confidentiality as their primary concern. Although these items were originally identified as separate items, when asked to rank order issues that need to be addressed as a team, they were collapsed into a single item.

The team appears to have high regard for management's commitment and dedication and generally believes that management cares about the employees but some practices have led to questions about trustworthiness and have led to changes in communication with management. This in turn has also led to deterioration in the team cohesion and motivation. The team recognizes a role it plays in changing this dynamic with one member stating that the work group just needs to "get over" issues such as the suspicion generated when managers close their doors.

Regarding the process: *"This is the first time since I've been here that anything has been done to help the department."* Positively referring to the process started by HR Representative and Management and culminating in the consultant's participation.

"This is the first time since I've been here that anything has been done to help the department." referring to the process started by HR Representative.

Select Comments:

Asking employees about others' job performance encourages playing a "tattle-tale" role and reduces trust.

The frequency of "closed door meetings," the door being closed all day reduces trust.

Employees feel stressed when asked to be "tattle-tales" on peers.

Managers identifying peers who give (personal or work related) information about the employee leads to questions about confidentiality.

There has been a history of both supervisors and employees talking behind each others' backs.

Honesty doesn't seem to be valued. Unspoken message is, "Don't complain."

Mistakes are brought up "over and over." Management talks about moving on but this gives the perception that they don't move on and it destroys trust. Don't want to tell about mistakes for fear of hearing about them over and over.

"The lack of confidentiality... encourages employees to "just do your job," or "go home, and look for another job."
—Employee

Recommendations (rank order):

1.   Management should adopt a policy of asking employees directly about issues and refrain from talking about employees inside or outside the department except as necessary for their job functions.

2.   Changes in how managers handle "closed door meetings" combined with employees "getting past" the past history would improve trust, respect, and confidentiality and greatly improve motivation. This can be accomplished by:

       ✓ scheduling (with identified topics for) these meetings (reduces suspicion)

       ✓ meeting just before or after work

       ✓ "going to lunch" to meet with employees

       ✓ partially closed door meetings among management when appropriate

       ✓ communicating if and when interruptions are allowed

3.   Personal issues—not work issues—shared with a manager should NOT be shared unless permission is given.

4.   Clarify roles/responsibilities for each manager (know which manager to take issues to based on job functions).

Select Comments:

Employee absences make the work fall onto the backup. This person then has two job functions to fulfill. Cross training so that tasks could be "divided up" among employees would help.

High turnover has led to higher stress and lower efficiency due to having to learn the functions of employees who leave.

Stress is increased by having to complete all job functions and at the same time train new employees.

Backing up a peer on a job that the employee has not performed for more than a year increases stress and errors.

The policy for taking breaks is unclear. Are no breaks allowed? 10 minute breaks? Does this include bathroom breaks? There have been mixed messages with statements like, "No one takes breaks. But you can."

Helping others with their workload is not encouraged.

Perceived that overtime is only approved on holiday weeks (straight time) and is thus based on cost, not the workload and need.

"Turnover has been a problem—I think it is 24 [employees] in three and a half years, this leads to a lot of stress and an increased workload."
"It [turnover] was better before... about three years ago."

Recommendations (rank order):

1. Have management sit with employee quarterly or twice annually to evaluate workload, learn the job's functions, and update the job description (with employee review).

2. Utilize Human Resources or an outside consultant to evaluate workload versus current FTEs and hire one or two new employees if warranted to help with training, cross training, and increased workload due to new accounts. Include an evaluation of the workload/error ratio.

3. Cross train employees to increase sense of team work and ability to share the workload: split up the back up responsibilities and prioritize by job task with each having one main back up plus others cross trained (for task #1: Bob then Mary then Jane; task #2 Jane then Bob then Joe).

4. Clarify use of time off—flex and incidental time—to support a sense of work-life balance without guilt or reprimands for its use.

Select Comments:

Having to train and at the same time doing your regular job increases job stress and lowers job satisfaction.

Turnover with no overlap on job functions increases stress and lowers morale.

Limited job shadowing lengthens the learning curve and increases errors.

Some employees do not get adequately trained in all areas and this lack of training leads to errors.

One long term employee stated that they still find things they weren't trained on and thus feels intimidated by the work. Also knows they will be blamed for mistakes made by trainees. Consequences need to be in place, but should be for "patterns or repeated errors" not lack of adequate training.

Employees "double checking" work have not been fully trained and don't know the job well enough to catch many potential errors.

Asking for help implies that an employee doesn't know their job and the message is that they "should know."

Employee absences make the work fall onto the backup. This person then has two job functions to fulfill. Cross training so that tasks could be "divided up" among employees would help.

"I've been working here longer than most and I still find things that I don't know [had to train themselves]—and I'm supposed to train the next person to do it... if the next employee doesn't get trained in some area then I will be blamed."

Recommendations (rank order):

1. Develop plan for job shadowing to cross-train new and existing employees.

2. Inform current employees about job postings before making them public.

3. Begin hiring process (such as developing a current job description) before employee leaves and before launching a new venture.

4. Budget for overlaps in a single job function to allow for training (like in the accounting area).

Select Comments:

The management team members are hard workers often working very late & many hours a week.

Very knowledgeable in some areas but don't know job functions in other areas so management can't help in training or providing assistance in many needed situations.

Would like to see the supervisor more in a supervisory role and less acting as a "direct service" employee.

The group had questions about the support the supervisor has received to fulfill the supervisor role. (Training? Comfort level as a supervisor? Confidence in having decisions supported? Confidence was viewed as better in the past.)

Information shared with one of the management team gets shared with the other who then calls the employee in to address.

Recommendations (rank order):

1. Develop a current job description and share it with the employees.

2. Complete timely reviews/evaluations for all positions (including management), tracking their completion, with HR to follow up if not completed on time.

3. Prioritize learning of other areas than their primary area of expertise.

4. Clarify supervisor/Department Head roles including responsibilities for job reviews.

5. Clarify employee/ supervisor role and tasks in primary area.

6. Like to see supervisor use "fact finding" and demonstrating leadership in decision making rather then taking every decision to the Department Head (has changed over past three years).

Select Comments:

Employees are often asked to evaluate peers' performance for job reviews; this leads to poor peer relations, low trust, and conflict if performance is not judged to be adequate.

Reprimands that should be between the supervisor and the employee(s) affected only have been shared with other employees—an example is when flex time was taken away and the notice was emailed to the entire workgroup. The issue was not addressed with the employee in a job review the same week, and the email split the work team.

Employees have questions about the role of the supervisor's position and wonder if job reviews have been completed for the management staff to help direct and guide their job functions.

"Asking employees to evaluate other team members' job performance leads to mistrust among team members, a lack of confidence in management's knowledge of employees' job functions, and an unwillingness to admit mistakes."

Recommendations (rank order):

1. Suggestion #1 under Workload—supervisor sitting with employee quarterly—will help in evaluating employees without asking peers to evaluate each other.

2. Suggestion #2 under Supervisor's Role—timely reviews—and suggestions #1 and #2 under Trust, Respect, and Confidentiality—direct communication and closed-door practices—can address concerns about reprimands.

Select Comments:

Employees have to answer for everything you do—even little things that are not critical.

Reminders are given for normal job functions—conveys lack of trust.

There is system of checking up on your work even if there have been no problems.

"I know that they are responsible for us doing our jobs and they have to answer for our mistakes... but when you are questioned over normal [routine] tasks and small things are treated like critical issues, you don't feel like they trust you to do the job." "It just makes you want to do your job [as opposed to achieving top performance] and leave."

Recommendations (rank order):

1. Demonstrate confidence and trust in the supervisor and employees.

2. Update job description for Department Head (who does extra tasks frequently) to increase efficiency for the department.

3. Clarify task responsibility for employees and management (example: delicate task of calling a widow about an account and payment plan).

4. Clarify critical tasks; not acting as if minor issues are major issues.

Sample D2:
Manufacturing Report: Demographics

Focus Group Demographic Data

Number of Participants by Plant

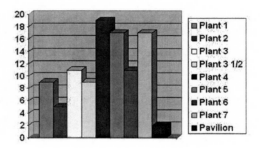

Gender By Percentage

Participants by Shift

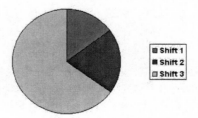

Sample D3: Leadership Report & Action Plan Meeting Agenda

Leadership Team Meeting Agenda

"Pity the leader caught between unloving critics and uncritical lovers." **John Gardner**

I. Brief Reactions/Feedback to Leadership from Sunday's Meeting

II. Issues to Address From the Meeting

    a. Continued Leadership Issuing from the Apology

        i. Are more apologies needed?

        ii. How does the congregation SEE the changes of a sorrowful heart?

        iii. How do we rebuild relationships & trust?

    b. Suggestions made that the Leadership Team should consider.

        i. Communication Opportunities

        ii. Involving leadership outside of the formal Leadership Team

    c. Follow-up Messages to Congregation

        i. i. Consultant

1. Apologies not my idea! Or just a step in the plan!

2. Thanks for attitude & suggestions to help Leadership.

3. Identify other opportunities for communication.

        ii. Pastor

1. _____

2. _____

     iii.   Leadership Team

1. _____

2. _____

III.   The Role of Leadership at this Church

    a.   Integrity is about "everything you do & how you treat me in the process"

    b.   What does a Pastor need from a Leadership Team?

    c.   What does the Leadership Team need form its Pastor?

    d.   Conflict and Leadership.

    e.   How do issues of Inclusion, Control, & Affection confound these issues?

IV.   Steps toward the April Meeting

    a.   How will the congregation see progress between now and then?

    b.   Who should run the meeting? Should this be shared?

    c.   _____

_____

"Outstanding leaders go out of their way to boost the self-esteem of their personnel. If people believe in themselves, it's amazing what they can accomplish."
—Sam Walton

"I suppose leadership at one time meant muscles; but today it means getting along with people."
—Mohandas K. Gandhi

Sample D4: Leadership Retreat PowerPoint Document

Human Systems Consultation, Inc.
Bryan G. Miller, Ph.D.

midlands church
... becoming like Christ

Leadership Retreat

Overview

◊ Format & Schedule

◊ What are the "take-aways" at the end of the day?

- Understanding your leadership strengths

- Identifying leadership challenges

- Identify roles for development of processes

- Begin definition of goals, processes, and rank ordering steps

◊ What if we find there are other steps to take?

◊ What MUST happen to succeed?

Goals: As Outlined by Midlands

◊ A plan & process for revitalizing ministry, increasing involvement & equipping leaders.

◊ A plan for communication.

◊ A plan to involve everyone in decisions & process.

◊ Leadership roles for shepherds.

Goals: Reformulated

◊ Two Broad Goals: (?)

- Roles for leadership.

- Processes for ministry involvement, communication, and equipping leaders.

Assessment & Leadership

◊ How can the assessment help Midlands reach its goals?

◊ Leaders will have more awareness and appreciation of their strengths

◊ Help align organizational tasks to strengths & interests

◊ Identify areas of need in overall leadership

◊ Utilize strengths to develop efficient plans & processes

◊ Assessment Limitations

◊ Only as good as the information provided

◊ Not an assessment of skills

◊ No inherent "good" or "bad" to the types and preferences

◊ Provides "hypotheses" to test with your own experiences

◊ Can be influenced by context

Traits of the MBTI & FIRO B

◊ To explore and expand understanding of your leadership style and your interactions with others

◊ Specifically how you are likely to engage in communication, problem solving, decision making & interpersonal relationships

◊ Two instruments from two theoretical and instrumentally different traditions give two views of your leadership style

MBTI & FIRO B: Leadership Report

◊ Highlights:

- Each person's strengths & blind spots
- Divergence in views, attitudes, values & behaviors
- Different operating styles
- Use of different leadership styles

The MBTI Type & Leadership

◊ Because understanding the assessment is part of the learning curve, building on concepts already "known" can increase the utility of the assessments

◊ MBTI is based on familiar concepts, the FIRO B Leadership Report expands this to increase the rigor of the evaluation and specifically targets leadership issues

The FIRO – B Leadership Report

◊ Leadership Report Overview:

- Overall Leadership Orientation
- Interpretation of FIRO B Results
- Interpretation of MBTI Results
- Interpersonal Relations
- Working with Groups & Other Leaders
- Power & Organizational Culture
- Dealing with Change & Stress
- Action Plan

Task: Record Keeping

◊ Use paper to keep notes on:

- Overall leadership orientation
- Interpersonal relations
- Working with Groups & Other Leaders
- Power & Organizational Culture
- Dealing with Change & Stress

◊ Record feedback from others

FIRO B: Leadership Orientation

◊ Focus: Identifying your broad leadership style and approach

◊ Strongest interpersonal need = Total Need Score

◊ Ties are rank ordered by Affection, Control, Inclusion based on theory

◊ Identify key words/phrases that characterize your leadership approach

◊ What themes emerge across the results?

◊ What terms are the weakest fit?

FIRO B: FIRO B Results

◊ Focus: 3 areas of Social Needs of Leadership/ Organizations and 2 orientations toward behavior

◊ Social Needs:

  • Inclusion (participation, recognition, belonging)

  • Control (power, authority, influence)

  • Affection (openness, warmth, closeness)

◊ Orientations toward Initiation of Behavior:

  • Expressed (you tend to initiate)

  • Wanted (hope others will initiate)

Record Keeping #2

◊ Add sections for:

  • Social needs I want to express

◊ Inclusion

◊ Control

◊ Affection

  • Social needs I want to receive

◊ Inclusion

◊ Control

◊ Affection

Clarifications
◊ High Inclusion/Low Affection: Friendly but not intimate, like a salesperson

◊ High Affection/Low Inclusion: Likes closeness but does not need to "bring people together" like a therapist

◊ Expressed/ Wanted Behaviors: Expressed = action toward others, Wanted = Passive acceptance of actions from others

FIRO B Results cont.
Total Scores
◊ Overall personal needs (corr. With E – I type)

◊ Compare Expressed/Wanted (action anxiety vs. dependence on others)

◊ Total Need Scores

   • Pattern of Need Fulfillment

◊ Low 0-2 = 'Not expressed" or "Not get"

◊ Medium 3-6 = "Sometimes express or get"

◊ High 7-9 = "Likely express or get"

   • Roles You Take On

◊ Clarifier

◊ Director

◊ Encourager

◊ Based on the results, what percentage of time would you be likely to spend in the three basic roles? (Clarifier, Director, Encourager)

◊ What are the benefits/dangers of spending too much time in any one role?

◊ How does this fit with the current organizational expectations?

Record Keeping #3

◊ Add "My preferred roles":

- Clarifier

- Director

- Encourager

FIRO B: Results

◊ What if your role activities are all high, medium or low?

◊ Risks:

- High (role confusion)

- Medium (excessive unpredictability)

- Low (perceived indifference)

◊ What about role conflicts?

- Are your roles in conflict with your needs?

- How does it fit within the leadership team?

FIRO B: MBTI Results
◊ Two poles on four personality dichotomies

Extraversion	--	Introversion
Sensing	--	Intuition
Thinking	--	Feeling
Judging	--	Perceiving

MBTI

Extraversion (E)
◊ Like variety and action

◊ Are often impatient with long, slow jobs

◊ Are interested in the activities of your work and in how other people do them

◊ Act quickly, sometimes without thinking

◊ When working on a task, find phone calls a welcome diversion

◊ Develop ideas through discussion

◊ Like having people around

Introversion (I)
◊ Seen as "reflective" or "reserved"

◊ Comfortable being alone and like things they can do on their own

◊ Prefer to know just a few people well

◊ Spend time reflecting and may not move into action quickly enough

◊ Get energy as they develop ideas internally

◊ Sometimes forget to check with the outside world to see if my ideas really fit the experience

Sensing (S)

◊ Remember events as snapshots of what actually happened

◊ Solve problems by working through facts until I understand the problem

◊ Pragmatic and look to the "bottom line"

◊ Start with facts and then form a big picture.

◊ Trust experience first and trust words and symbols less

◊ Sometimes pay so much attention to facts, either present or past, that I miss new possibilities

Intuition (N)

◊ Like solving new, complex problems

◊ Enjoy learning a new skill more than using it

◊ May follow your inspirations, good or bad

◊ May make errors of fact

◊ Like to do things with an innovative bent

◊ Like to present an overview of your work first

◊ Prefer change, sometimes radical, to continuation of what is

◊ Usually proceed in bursts of energy

Thinking (T)

◊ Use logical analysis to reach conclusions

◊ Can work without harmony

◊ May hurt people's feelings without knowing it

◊ Tend to decide impersonally, sometimes paying insufficient attention to people's wishes

◊ Tend to be firm minded and can give criticism when appropriate

◊ Look at the principles in the situation

◊ Feel rewarded when job is done well

Feeling (F)

◊ Use values to reach conclusions

◊ Work best in harmony with others

◊ Enjoy pleasing people, even in unimportant things

◊ Let decisions be influenced by your own and others' likes and dislikes

◊ Are sympathetic and dislike, even avoid, telling people unpleasant things

◊ Look at the underlying values in the situation

◊ Feel rewarded when people's needs are met

Judging (J)

◊ Work best when you can plan your work and follow your plan

◊ Like to get things settled and finished

◊ May not notice new things that need to be done

◊ Tend to be satisfied once you reach a decision on a thing, situation, or person

◊ Reach closure by deciding quickly

◊ Seek structure and schedules

◊ Use lists to prompt action on specific tasks

Perceiving (P)

◊ Enjoy flexibility in your work

◊ Like to leave things open for last-minute changes

◊ May postpone unpleasant tasks

◊ May be curious and welcome new views on a thing, situation, or person

◊ Postpone decisions while searching for options

◊ Adapt well to changing situations and feel restricted without change

◊ Use lists to remind yourself of all the things you have to do someday

◊ Extraverted Sensing

- Allen

◊ Extraverted Intuition

- Bill, Jim, Tom

◊ Extraverted Feeling

- Mike

◊ Extraverted Thinking

- Ken

High Level Types

ENFP (Bill, Tom)

◊ Enthusiastic, idealistic, and creative. Able to do almost anything that interests them. Great people skills. Need to live life in accordance with their inner values. Excited by new ideas, but bored with details. Open-minded and flexible, with a broad range of interests and abilities.

ENTP (Jim)

◊ Creative, resourceful, and intellectually quick. Good at a broad range of things. Enjoy debating issues, and may be into "one-up-manship." They get very excited about new ideas and projects, but may neglect the more routine aspects of life. Generally outspoken and assertive. They enjoy people and are stimulating company. Excellent ability to understand concepts and apply logic to find solutions.

ENFJ (Mike)

◊ Popular and sensitive, with outstanding people skills. Externally focused, with real concern for how others think and feel. Usually dislike being alone. They see everything from the human angle, and dislike impersonal analysis. Very effective at managing people issues, and leading group discussions. Interested in serving others, and probably place the needs of others over their own needs.

ENTJ (Ken)

◊ Assertive and outspoken - they are driven to lead.
Excellent ability to understand difficult organizational
problems and create solid solutions. Intelligent
and well-informed, they usually excel at public
speaking. They value knowledge and competence,
and usually have little patience with inefficiency or
disorganization.

ISFP (Allen)

◊ Quiet, serious, sensitive and kind. Do not like conflict,
and not likely to do things which may generate
conflict. Loyal and faithful. Extremely well-developed
senses, and aesthetic appreciation for beauty. Not
interested in leading or controlling others. Flexible
and open-minded. Likely to be original and creative.
Enjoy the present moment.

And . . .

Because everything ultimately comes back to this question ...

◊ "How does it connect to Star Trek?"

◊ Presenting... Your MBTI type as a Trekkie.

MBTI & Star Trek (www.wischik.com/ damon/texts/myersbriggs.html)

◊ ESTJ: Lt. Cm. Riker

◊ ESTP: Jordi LaForge

◊ ENFJ: Counselor Troi

◊ ENTJ: Q

◊ INTJ: Spock

◊ ISTP: Wesley Crusher

◊ INFJ: Benjamin Sisko

◊ INTJ: Capt. Pickard

◊ ESFJ: Dr. McCoy

◊ ESFP: Capt. Janeway

◊ ENFP: Capt. Kirk

◊ ENTP: Harry Kim

◊ ISFJ: Chakotay

◊ ISFP: EMH (Doctor)

◊ INFP: Garak & Kes

◊ INTP: Worf

E & I Working Together

◊ Meetings

◊ Work Environment

◊ Incentives

◊ Role Assignment

S & N Working Together

◊ Process, Procedures and Work Flow Design

◊ Strategic Planning

◊ Workspace Design and Tools of the Trade

T & F Working Together

◊ Feeling Valued and Appreciated

◊ Accepting Criticism

◊ Problem Solving

◊ Delivering Bad News

◊ Working Environment

J & P Working Together

◊ Working with Policies and Procedures

◊ Decision Making

◊ Punctuality

◊ Change Management

Integrating FIRO B & MBTI Results

◊ Overall Need compared to E- I

◊ High/Low FIRO to MBTI

◊ Any other areas of convergence?

◊ Areas of divergence?

◊ Remember:

- Two different theories/ traditions

- FIRO = social needs, MBTI adds cognitive

- FIRO strength of needs, MBTI preferences
- FIRO uni-polar, MBTI bipolar
- Different scales, language, score weightings, etc.

FIRO B: Interpersonal Relations

◊ Purpose of this Section:

- Linkages between interaction approach & visibility as a leader
- Explore "first impressions"

◊ Interactions and Your Leadership

◊ What You Show First in Leadership

FIRO B: Groups & Other Leaders

◊ Purpose

- Explore leadership in team settings
- Reactions to others' attempts to lead & influence (low scores = more sensitive to)
- Note differences in leadership style and how you like to be lead

◊ Talk About Teams You have Found Most Rewarding

◊ How You Work in a Team

◊ What You Expect from Other Leaders

FIRO B: Power & Culture

◊ Purpose:

- Introduce the leader's orientation to power & their influence on organizational culture

- Note differences between preferred relating and political energies

- Explore match of current and preferred environments

◊ Describe the Power & Culture of the Organization

◊ Your Bases of Power & Influence

◊ Your Influence on Organizational Culture

- Note: Long term & Short term emphasis may be different (var. in FIRO & MBTI)

Typology: Power & Culture

◊ Mitroff & Kilmann (1975); Hirsh (1992) suggest the following relationships:

- STs establish Hierarchical structures

- SFs structures are Fraternal

- NFs value Collegial structures

- NT like Entrepreneurial structures

FIRO B: Change & Stress

◊ Purpose: Identify resources & pressure points during change & stress

◊ What are the current stressors and challenges?

◊ The additive effect of stress.

◊ What strengths are you applying to these stressors & challenges.

◊ Examine the column of strengths – what other resources can you use?

◊ Other areas to explore:

- Overall Leadership Orientation (Change Approach)

- Organizational Role Preferences

- How you work in a Team

- What you expect from other Leaders

- Ways of influencing others (Bases of Power and Influence)

- Resources/strengths are NOT limitless!

FIRO B: Action Plan

◊ Purpose: Continued development as a leader

◊ What findings did you find most helpful?

◊ Based on your MBTI Type, what methods of learning are most likely to aid your development?

◊ How will your development help in the continuing work of your leadership?

Organizational Needs: Roles

◊ Affection

- Openness

- Warmth

- Closeness

◊ Control

- Power

- Authority

- Influence

◊ Inclusion

- Participation

- Recognition

- Belonging

Defining Goals for Organizational Processes

◊ Elevator Ride: What is Midlands?

◊ What is the Midlands' Brand? What are we known for?

◊ What are we good at?

◊ What do we not want to be?

◊ Where are our opportunities?

Starting with the End in Mind

◊ If our work today is very successful, what will be have happened or not happened when we are done?

◊ If the goals are accomplished, how will we know?

◊ Is this vision realistic? Too modest? Too ambitious?

◊ Let's start by defining problem statements

Discussion Rules

◊ Problem specification now, goal setting/decisions later

◊ 50% agreement for problem to be submitted

◊ Refer to individuals by titles not names

◊ Recommendations do not require agreement

◊ Discussion is confidential

Problem Statements

◊ Who experiences the problem?

◊ What factors contribute to the problem?

◊ Why is it a problem for the church?

◊ When is it a problem?

◊ Where is the problem located?

◊ How does the problem affect your work and your feelings?

Sample Problem Statement

◊ Problem: The secretarial staff is experiencing low morale.

◊ Recommendations:

1. Have more social events.

2. Develop a career path.

Problem Statement & Recommendation Checks

◊ Is the statement clear and specific?

◊ Do recommendations address problems or are they problems themselves?

◊ Have all group members contributed to the solutions?

Rank Ordering Importance

◊ One challenge is determining what should be done first, second, etc.

◊ Resources are limited!

◊ Intuitives tend to over estimate their abilities (grand ideas) and must check their ideas with the realities of processes

The Five Interrogatives & Goals

◊ Have we answered the following?

- Who?

- What?

- When?

- Where?

- Why?

- How?

How Will We Know It Happened?

◊ One more check:

◊ Have we answered how we will know if it has happened?

◊ Staying on Track

◊ How will we sustain progress?

◊ Measure progress?

◊ Continued planning and adaptations?

Overview of Process & Outcomes

◊ Let's review what we hoped to accomplish and evaluate the process

◊ Did we achieve the original goal?

◊ If not, what influenced a change in the process?

◊ Was it a natural or useful development?

◊ What would improve the process?

Human Systems Consultation, Inc.
Bryan G. Miller, Ph.D.

Appendix E:

Business Documents: Expense Tracking, Invoices, Billing, Time Sheets

---

More examples at
www.hsystemsconsulting.com/resources.php.

Example E1:
Excel Spreadsheet of Expenses

Date	Hours Worked	Mileage (Miles)	Description	Hrs to Bill	Cost	Amoun Billed
26-Jan	3		Meeting	0	$	$
27-Jan	5		Proposal Writing	0	$	$
14-Feb	3		Review Tapes	0	$	$
16-Feb	2.5		Meetings Frank Deb	1	$	$
17-Feb	4		Meetings Frank Deb	4	$	$
18-Feb	2		Contract, Phone calls, E-mails	1	$	$
23-Feb	3	12	Interviews	3	$	$
1-Mar			Billing		$	$
1-Mar	7	92	Interviews	7	$	$
3-Mar	7	73	Interviews	5	$	$
8-Mar	2	5	Interviews	1	$	$
9-Mar	4	62	Meetings -Frank, L. Team	4	$	$
16-Mar	2.5	58	L. Team Meeting	2	$	$
18-Mar	2.25		Meeting Frank	2	$	$
20-Mar	2		Phone, E-mail Apology	0	$	$
26-Mar	1		Apology Draft	1	$	$
27-Mar	1		Apology Rewrite, E-mails, Phone	0	$	$
29-Mar	3		Congregational Meeting	1.5	$	$
30-Mar	5	58	L. Team Meeting	4	$	$
1-Apr			Billing		$	$
2-Apr	2		Meeting Frank	1.5	$	$

Date	Hours Worked	Mileage (Miles)	Description	Hrs to Bill	Cost	Amount Billed
-Apr	2	58	Congregational Mtg.	2	$	$
-Apr	2	58	L. Team Meeting	2	$	$
May			Billing		$	$
-May	2		Meeting Frank	2	$	$
-May	3		L. Team Meeting	3	$	$
Jun			Billing		$	$
Jun	2		L. Team Meeting	2	$	$
Jul			Billing		$	$
			Total		$	$

Sample E2: Basic Bill

Human Systems Consultation, Inc.

123 County Road

Cityville, ST 54321

Phone Number

EIN:

Consultant: Bryan G. Miller, Ph.D.

Date of Service:	Activity	Hours Billed	Charge
March 1	Interviews	7	$
March 3	Interviews	5	$
March 8	Interviews	1	$
March 9	Meetings –Pastor, Leadership Team	4	$
March 16	Leadership Team Meeting	2	$
March 18	Meeting Pastor	2	$
March 26	Congregation Note Draft	1	$
March 27	Draft Rewrite, E-mails, Phone	0	$
March 29	Congregational Meeting	1.5	$
March 30	Leadership Team Meeting	4	$
March Totals		27.5	$

Hours Billed: 27.5 (Excludes mileage, planning, administrative work on behalf of Team)

Cost Per Hour: $ XXX.00

....

Total Due Upon Receipt: $ XXXX.00

....

Please return with Payment:

Send payment to:

Local Church   Human Systems Consultation, Inc.
Street Street   123 Country Road
Metro, NE   Cityville, ST ZIP

Billing Dates: March, 2009
Total Due: $XXXX.00

Sample E3: Time Sheet

Human Systems Consulting   TIME SHEET
"Maximizing Human Capital"

247 Cheney Rd.

Middleton, NE 68111

Employee Name: Title: Office Administrator

Employee Number: 16   Status: Part-time

Department: Supervisor: Dr. Bryan G. Miller

Date	Start Time	End Time	Regular Hrs.	Overtime Hrs.	Total Hrs.
		MONTHLY TOTALS:			

Employee Signature: Date:

Supervisor Signature: Date:

References

Additional resources and "recent finds" are available at www.hsystemsconsulting.com/resources.php.

Appreciative Inquiry Commons Online. (2010). http://appreciativeinquiry.case. edu.

Bateson, Gregory. (1972). *Steps to an Ecology of the Mind.* New York: Ballantine Books.

Beck, A. T. (1967). Depression: Causes and Treatment. Philadelphia: University of Philadelphia Press.

Beck, A. T., Rush, A. J., Shaw, B. F. & Emery, G. (1979). Cognitive Therapy of Depression. New York: Guilford.

Bernard, H. Russell. (1995). *Research Methods in Anthropology* (2nd ed.). London: AltaMira Press.

Biech, Elaine. (2001). The Consultant's Quick Start Guide: An Action Plan for Your First Year in Business. New York: Jossey-Bass/Pfeiffer.

Biswas, Sugata, & Twitchell, Daryl. (2002). *Management Consulting: A Complete Guide to the Industry* (2nd ed.). New York: Wiley.

Block, Peter. (1999). *Flawless Consulting: A Guide to Getting your Expertise Used* (2nd ed.). New York: Wiley: Jossey-Bass/Pfeiffer.

Bloomberg Businessweek. (2002). www.businessweek.com/chapter/degeus.htm.

Boverie, P. E. (1991). Human Systems Consultant: Using Family Therapy in Organizations. *Family Therapy,* 18, 61-71.

Brown-Volkman, Deborah. (2003). *Four Steps to Building a Profitable Coaching Practice: A Complete Marketing Resource Guide for Coaches.* Lincoln, NE: iUniverse.

Capelle, Ronald G. (1979). *Changing Human Systems.* Toronto: International Human Systems Institute.

Cooperrider, D., & Sekerka, L. (2006). *Toward a Theory of Positive Organizational Change.* Organization Development: In Gallos, Joan (Ed.), Organization Development. A Jossey-Bass Reader. San Francisco: Jossey-Bass/Wiley.

Cooperrider, D., & Whitney, D. (2005). *Appreciative Inquiry: A Positive Revolution in Change.* San Francisco: Berrett-Koehler Publishers.

Deming, W. E. (1986). Out of the Crisis. Cambridge: MIT Press.

Deming, W. E. (2000). The New Economics for Industry, Government, Education (2nd ed.). Cambridge: MIT Press.

Drucker, P. F. (1954). Practice of Management. New York: Harper & Row.

Edwards, Paul, & Edwards, Sarah. (1998). *Getting Business to Come to You* (2nd ed.). New York: Putnam.

Fetsch, R. J., & Zimmerman, T. S. (1999). Marriage and Family Consultation with Ranch and Farm Families: An Empirical Family Case Study. *Journal of Marriage and Family Therapy,* 25(4), 485-501.

Flaherty, J. (1999). Coaching: Evoking Excellence in Others. Burlington, Mass.: Elsevier (USA).

Fleming, Quentin J. (2000). *Keep the Family Baggage Out of the Family Business.* New York: Fireside.

Friedman, E. (1986). Emotional Process in the Marketplace: The Family Therapist as Consultant with Work Systems. In L. Wynne, S. McDaniel, & T. Weber (Eds.), *Systems Consultation: A New Perspective in Family Therapy* (pp. 398-422). New York: Guilford Press.

Gersick, Kelin, Davis, John A., McCollom, Hampton & Lansberg, Ivan. (1997). *Generation to Generation: Life Cycles of the Family Business.* Boston: Harvard Business School Press.

Gordon, Grant, & Nicholson, Nigel. (2008). *Family Wars: Classic Conflicts in Family Business and How to Deal with Them.* Philadelphia: Kogan Page Limited.

Hamper, Robert J., & Baugh, L. Sue. (1995). *Handbook for Writing Proposals.* Chicago: NTC Business Books.

Hilburt-Davis, Jane, & Dyer, W. Gibb. (2003). *Consulting to Family Businesses.* San Francisco: Wiley.

Holtz, Herman. (1993). *How to Succeed as an Independent Consultant.* New York: Wiley.

Holtz, Herman. (1994). *The Business Plan Guide for Independent Consultants.* New York: Wiley.

Horan, Jim. (2006). The One Page Business Plan for the Professional Consultant. Berkeley, Calif.: The One Page Business Plan Company.

Institute of Management Consultants USA online. www.imcusa.org.

Jolles, Robert L. (2001). *How to Run Seminars and Workshops* (3rd ed.). New York: Wiley.

Kempa, Sheila, & White, Randall P. (2002). The Effectiveness of Executive Coaching: What We Know and What We Still Need to Know. In Lowman, Rodney L., (ed.). *Handbook of Organizational Psychology.* San Francisco: Jossey-Bass.

Keoughan, P., & Joanning, H. (1996). Getting Down to Business: From Therapist to Consultant. *Family Therapy News,* 16-28.

Keoughan, P., & Joanning, H. (1997). Getting Down to Business: Human Systems Consulting. Ankeny, Iowa: Human Systems Consultants, Inc.

Kvale, Steiner. (1996). *Interviews.* Thousand Oaks: Sage.

Lencioni, P. (1998). The Five Temptations of a CEO. San Fransico: Wiley & Sons.

Lencioni, P. (2000). The Four Obsessions of an Extraordinary Executive. San Francisco: Jossey-Bass/Wiley.

Lencioni, P. (2002). The Five Dysfunctions of a Team. San Francisco: Jossey-Bass/Wiley.

Lencioni, P. (2004). Death by Meeting. San Francisco: Jossey-Bass/Wiley.

Lincoln, Yvonne, & Guba, Egon. (1985). *Naturalistic Inquiry.* New York: Sage.

Lowman, Rodney (ed.). (2002). *Handbook of Organizational Consulting Psychology.* San Francisco: Jossey-Bass.

Lukaszewski, J. E. (1988). Behind the Throne: How to Coach and Counsel Executives. *Training and Development Journal,* 42(10), 32-35.

Martin, Iris. (1996). *From Couch to Corporation: Becoming a Successful Corporate Therapist.* New York: Wiley.

Maslow, A. H. (1943). A Theory of Human Motivation. *Psychological Review,* 50(4), 370-96

Matheny, Aaron Clayton, & Zimmerman, Toni Schindler. (2001). The Application of Family Systems Theory to Organizational Consultation: A Content Analysis. *The American Journal of Family Therapy,* 29, 421-433.

Mayo, Elton. (1933). *The Human Problems of an Industrialized Civilisation.* New York: MacMillan.

McClendon, R., & Kadis, L.B. (1991). Family Therapists and Family Business: A View of the Future. *Contemporary Family Therapy: An International Journal,* 13(6), 641-651.

McClendon, Ruth, & Kadis, Leslie. (2004). *Reconciling Relationships and Preserving the Family Business.* Routledge.

McDowell, Teresa. (1999). Systems Consultation and Head Start: An Alternative to Traditional Family Therapy. *Journal of Marital and Family Therapy,* 25 (2),155-168.

McGovern, J., et al. (2001). Maximizing the Impact of Executive Coaching. *The Manchester Review,* 6 (1), 3-11.

Morgan, Howard, Harkins, Phil, & Goldsmith, Marshall (eds.). (2005). *The Art and Practice of Leadership Coaching.* New York: Wiley.

Morrell, M., & Chapperell, S. (2002). Shackelton's Way: Leadership Lessons from the Great Antarctic Explorer. New York: Penguin Books.

Mullis, Darrell, & Orloff, Judith. (1998). *The Accounting Game: Basic Accounting Fresh from the Lemonade Stand.* Naperville, Ill.: Educational Discoveries, Inc.

Munsterberg, Hugo. (1913). *Psychology and Industrial Efficiency.* New York: Houghton Mifflin.

O'Neill, Beth. (2007). *Executive Coaching with Backbone and Heart.* San Francisco: Jossey-Bass/Wiley.

Peters, T. J., & Waterman, Jr., R. H. (1982). In Search of Excellence. New York: Warner Books, Inc.

Salant, P., and Dillman, D.A. (1994), *How to Conduct Your Own Survey.* New York: Wiley.

Scannell, Edward. (1980). *Games Trainers Play.* New York: McGraw-Hill.

Schein, Edgar H. (1980). *Organizational Psychology* (3rd ed.). Prentice Hall Foundations of Modern Psychology Series, Richard S. Lazarus (series editor). Englewood Cliffs, NJ: Prentice-Hall.

Schley, B. (2005). Why Johnny Can't Brand: Rediscovering the Lost Art of the Big Idea. New York: Penguin Group.

Sears, Richard, Rudisill, John, & Mason-Sears, Carrie. (2006). *Consultation Skills for Mental Health Professionals.* New York: Wiley.

Senge, Peter. (1990). *The Fifth Discipline: The Art & Practice of the Learning Organization.* New York: Doubleday.

Senge, Peter. (1994). *The Fifth Discipline Fieldbook.* New York: Doubleday.

Shenson, Howard. (1989). The Consultant's Guide to Proposal Writing. Chicago: H. L. Shenson.

Shenson, Howard, & Nicholas, Ted. (1997). *The Complete Guide to Consulting Success* (3rd ed.). Chicago: Dearborn Financial Publishing, Inc.

Sheth, J., & Sobel, A. (2000). Clients for Life: Evolving from an Expert for Hire to an Extraordinary Advisor. New York: Fireside.

Shook, L. (1985). Family Therapy Consultation and Organizational Change. *Journal of Strategic and Systemic Therapies*, 4, 8-14.

Silberman, Mel (ed.). (2001). *The Consultant's Tool Kit*. New York: McGraw Hill.

Sue, Valerie M., & Ritter, Lois A. (2007). *Conducting Online Surveys*. Los Angeles: Sage.

Taylor, Fredrick W. (1911). *The Principles of Scientific Management*. New York: Harper Brothers.

Tobias, Lester. L. (1990). *Psychological Consulting to Management: A Clinician's Perspective*. New York: Brunner/Mazel.

Trist, E., & Bamforth, K. (1951). Some Social and Psychological Consequences of the Longwall Method of Coal Getting. Human Relations 4: 3–38

Vollman, Thomas, Berry, William, Whybark, David Clay, & Jacobs, F. Robert. (2004). *Manufacturing Planning and Control Systems for Supply Chain Management: The Definitive Guide for Professionals*. New York: McGraw-Hill.

Von Bertalannfy, Ludwig (1968). General Systems Theory: Foundations, Development, Applications. New York: George Braziller, Inc.

Weiss, Alan. (2002) *Value Based Fees: How to Charge and Get What You're Worth*. San Francisco: Jossey-Bass/Pfeiffer.

Weiss, Alan. (2003). *Million Dollar Consulting* (3rd ed.). New York: McGraw-Hill.

Wiess, Alan. (2004). *Getting Started in Consulting* (2nd ed.). New York: Wiley.

Weiss, Alan. (2006). *Million Dollar Consulting Toolkit*. New York: Wiley.

Witherspoon, R., & White, R. P. (1996). Executive Coaching: A Continuum of Roles. *Consulting Psychology Journal: Practice and Research*, 48, 124-133.

Wynne, L.,McDaniel, S., & Weber, T. (Eds.). (1986). *Systems Consultation: A New Perspective for Family Therapy*. New York: Guilford Press.

Young, Jeffery. (1999). Cognitive Therapy for Personality Disorders: A Schema-Focused Approach (3rd ed.). Sarasota, Fla.: Professional Resource Press.

About the Author

D r. Bryan G. Miller is the President of Human Systems Consulting, Inc. (HSC). HSC was created to provide professional consulting, training, and education services on topics related to Human Systems—including systems of employees and families. HSC builds upon Dr. Miller's unique experience as a consultant, clinician, professor, researcher, and administrator to improve the functioning of these human systems.

Dr. Miller has worked as a business consultant, therapist, professor, researcher, and administrator since 1989. Dr. Miller's experience has included working with local, national, and international businesses as a consultant in areas as diverse as agriculture, manufacturing, banking, churches, and social service agencies. Previously, Dr. Miller worked with families as a therapist in venues such as a children's psychiatric hospital, a residential program, school-based programs, and in outpatient settings. Dr. Miller also supervised and administered family-based programs for more than ten years, including as an Executive Director.

Dr. Miller has been married to Amy (Young) Miller since 1981 and has six children. Currently, he is President of Human Systems Consulting, Inc., is an Associate Professor with Amridge University of Montgomery, Alabama, and also maintains a limited private practice with the Behavioral Pediatric and Family Therapy Program in Lincoln, Nebraska.

The "adoptive" father of three geese, seventeen ducks, forty-fifty chickens, five cats, two dogs, one parakeet, one horse, and forty to fifty thousand bees—as of last count, Dr. Miller can be reached at 4501 S. 70th St., Lincoln, NE 68516; (402) 641-3559.

E-mail: bryan@hsystemsconsulting.com
Web: www.hsystemsconsulting.com

Index

W

Y